LIFE WITH
THE PIONEERS

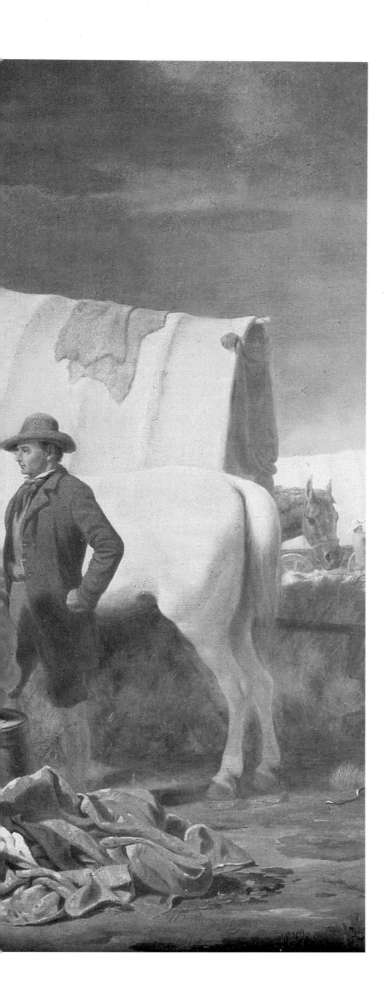

LIFE
WITH THE
PIONEERS

Reader's
Digest

Published by

THE READER'S DIGEST ASSOCIATION LIMITED

London   New York   Sydney
Montreal   Cape Town

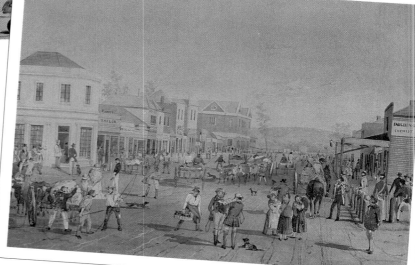

THE LONG ROAD Above: An 1802 painting showing a Boer family halting for the night.

DOWNTOWN Right: A view of Adelaide in 1845 gives no indication of its subsequent development into a thriving city.

LIFE WITH THE PIONEERS
Edited and designed by Toucan Books Limited
Sole author: Richard Tames

First edition copyright © 1996
The Reader's Digest Association Limited,
Berkeley Square House, Berkeley Square, London W1X 6AB

Copyright © 1996
Reader's Digest Association Far East Limited
Philippines copyright © 1996
Reader's Digest Association Far East Limited

All rights reserved
No part of this book may be reproduced, stored in a retrieval system, or transmitted in any form or by any means, electronic, electrostatic, magnetic tape, mechanical, photocopying, recording or otherwise, without permission in writing from the publishers.

® Reader's Digest, The Digest and the Pegasus logo are registered trademarks of The Reader's Digest Association, Inc, of Pleasantville, New York, USA

Printing and binding: Printer Industria Gráfica S.A., Barcelona
Separations: Grafiscan, Verona, Italy
Paper: Perigord-Condat, France

ISBN 0 276 42135 3

Page 1: SELF-SUFFICIENCY Crossing the plains with a handcart, pioneer life was reduced to the barest essentials. Men provided their own transport, defence and food supply.

Pages 2–3: VOICE OF EXPERIENCE North American pioneers in city clothes listen respectfully to the pronouncements of a leather-clad prairie guide.

Front cover (clockwise from top left): American pioneers; early pioneering family; fiddler; quinine bottle; wheelbarrow; Union Pacific poster; settler's home.

Back cover (clockwise from top left): Trading token; log cabin; San Gabriel Mission; snow shoes; American pioneer.

CONTENTS

FARAWAY PLACES The spread of elementary schooling increased knowledge of a wider, ever-growing world.

WELCOME WAGON Passengers landing at the port in Buenos Aires being ferried ashore in high-wheeled carts.

FALSE FINERY Settlers' status and wealth was denoted by their European clothes, often adopted by native peoples who sought to emulate them.

SHEFFIELD'S BEST

Our Set contains—

26-in. Hand Saw.	Mallet.
12-in. Back Saw.	Axe, handled.
Jack Plane.	Hammer.
Smooth Plane.	Spokeshave.
10-in. Brace.	Glue Pot and Brush,
Set of Bits.	3 Gimlets.
Walnut Square.	3 Bradawls.
4 Firmer Chisels.	Bradpunch.
3 Handled Gouges.	Marking Awl.
Large Turnscrew.	2 Files.
2-foot Rule.	Canvas-lined Bass.

Every Tool is Warranted.

CUTTING EDGE The introduction of cheap, well-made hand tools (above) speeded up work and made the lives of the pioneers much easier.

FREEDOM TRAIL? As a punishment, Tasmanian convicts were forced to routemarch while carrying heavy loads.

PERILS OF PIONEERING

The lure of land, the promise of freedom and the hope of a better life

drew millions from the Old World – to face challenges of

disappointment, disease and disaster.

PIONEERING WAS a dangerous enterprise. If the earliest settlers thought they had only to occupy a land and subjugate its inhabitants, it was a misjudgment that was to cost many lives.

The first 'successful' English colony in North America was Jamestown, Virginia, settled from 1607 onwards. However, within a period of 20 years, six-sevenths of the people who had emigrated there had died – most would have stood a better chance of survival in a battle.

Two hundred years later, colonies of Europeans were still clinging to the seaboards of North and South America, Australia, New Zealand and southern Africa, while the inland regions remained largely unexplored, their resources untapped, their native population unconfined.

GOOD HOPE? Cartoonist George Cruikshank satirises the glamorised options presented to would-be emigrants by Foreign Minister Castlereagh.

ON BOARD Thomas Baines based his painting of the landing of settlers at Algoa Bay, South Africa on eyewitness accounts. Right: Conditions were cramped below deck on a troopship bound for the Cape in 1819.

By 1815, two nations had emerged as Europe's major powers: France which, in its revolutionary decade (1792–1802), had proclaimed human rights and equality for all; and Britain which, having conceived the Industrial Revolution, was promising unique opportunities for production and prosperity. Together, they initiated the expansion of Europe's settlements overseas, eventually turning each of the territories into powerful and independent nations.

JOURNEY INTO THE UNKNOWN

Europe's dispossessed peasants, bankrupt traders, redundant craftsmen, discharged soldiers, religious eccentrics, exhausted servant girls, and exploited factory hands all believed that life in the new territories offered much that the Old World had denied them – land and a healthier and more prosperous future for themselves and their children.

Labour-starved governments in the receiving countries, well-intentioned philanthropists and self-interested land speculators, steamship and railroad companies all churned out literature to encourage immigration. Benjamin Franklin summarised their message with breezy irony: 'The only encouragements we hold out to strangers are – a good climate, fertile soil, wholesome air and water, plenty of provisions, good pay for labour, kind neighbours, good laws, a free government and a hearty welcome.' However, unless potential emigrants had some capital, they could not afford the outward voyage – the only alternatives being transportation as criminals or dissidents, or through being subsidised by a charity.

In 1816, 40 years after the Declaration of Independence, the United States claimed sovereignty over about two-thirds of its ultimate national territory. At the time the heartland, destined to become the source of the nation's sustenance, was considered nothing more than a sterile waste – 'the Great American Desert'.

Canada, as 'British North America', consisted of various separate colonies which, like their independent cousins in the south, continued to look to Britain, rather than to the west, for the source of their prosperity.

HOME COMFORTS   This Nebraska 'soddy', a house made from sods of turf, is typical of the first homes of many settlers.

In South America the colonies of Spain and Portugal, established even earlier than those to the north, were in the process of throwing off imperial rule. Australia – in effect, New South Wales and Tasmania – was still primarily a convict settlement, but its ex-convict inhabitants were swiftly asserting their rights as free men and already regarding subsequent arrivals as their social inferiors. New Zealand, familiar to few but sealers, whalers and missionaries, beckoned as a fertile, forested land ripe for settlement.

In southern Africa, the British had begun to impose themselves on the long-settled Dutch. But neither nation had, as yet, ventured into the country's vast interior. Shaka, a Zulu military genius, was building an empire which would, in 1879, throw the entire southern half of the continent into turmoil. The Barbary coast of North Africa was still the unmolested lair of marauding privateers and the home of a stable, prosperous Muslim culture.

In the century after Napoleon's defeat in 1815, all these countries were to come even more firmly under the control of people of European stock.

CROSSING THE GREAT DIVIDE

British emigrants to Australia, New Zealand and Canada travelled under official supervision, protected by regulations to safeguard their health, safety and comfort. Even convict ships were rigorously inspected for seaworthiness (in theory, at least) and subject to conditions regarding the prisoners' diet, exercise and living space. This was in the contractor's interest, too, as fees were docked in proportion to the number of deaths occurring in transit. The much larger North American traffic was, by contrast, a free-for-all. Ships bringing cotton and timber from America, or lumber from Canada, needed a return cargo. Failing more profitable freight, steerage passengers – those who travelled in the hold of the ship, rather than in cabins – were regarded as an acceptable alternative. Fares fell substantially, from £12 in 1816 to just over £3 by 1846 (in 1816, £1 a week was considered a good wage for an adult factory worker). Depending on size, the ships could carry anything from a few dozen passengers to up to 200.

Most British transatlantic emigrant vessels were classified at Lloyd's as 'third-class' – unfit for cargoes liable to water damage, and inadequate for voyages out of European waters. Accommodation and facilities were primitive. Few ships had privies,

UNWELCOME VISITOR   A snake disrupts an Australian party. In frontier country, immigrants tried to maintain European manners, clothing and customs.

NATURAL DISASTER This large hotel survived the eruption of New Zealand's Mount Tarawera in 1886; of the 70 houses nearby, only five were still habitable afterwards.

peppermint to ward off seasickness, or to provoke it by chewing toasted bacon fat or swallowing sea water. Neither method was particularly effective.

Nine out of ten ships had no medically qualified personnel. In 1847 and those that did have them had, on average, only one for every hundred passengers. American ships, on the other hand, were built specifically for passengers and by the 1840s they were carrying twice as many emigrants as British vessels. This did not mean that the voyage was any less hazardous. Between 1847 and 1853, for example, 59 ships were lost on the Atlantic run through storms. Passengers were told to dose themselves with opium or alone, one in six of the 106 812 migrants who sailed for British North America died, mostly victims of typhus or dysentery. Matters slowly improved: during the 1840s the sale of spirits on board ship

FRONTIER SOCIALISM Barn-raisings, as in this scene from Ohio in 1888, were often social events. Fiercely independent farmers cheerfully worked together on tasks beyond the resources of a single family.

was banned; emigration officers were empowered to judge the competence of crews; steerage passenger space was increased from 10 to 12 sq ft (0.93 to 1.10 sq m) per person; and single men and women were no longer allowed to berth together. In 1852, ships were required to have a sickbay and at least four privies. Dangerous cargoes were forbidden on passenger-carrying ships, and cooked food had to be available for passengers every day. Three years later, meat and vegetables were obligatory, added to the standard fare of biscuit, rice, oatmeal and molasses. Further improvements were made from the 1850s onwards, when steamships began to replace sail – not least because the duration of the average Atlantic crossing fell from 35 days to 15 or less.

THE PROMISED LAND?

A common experience of Europeans in widely contrasting environments was backbreaking labour and domestic drudgery – the respective lot of most men and women. Others found to their cost that past oppressors, such as the feudal landlord and the priest, were replaced by new ones, including bankers, railroad companies, cattle barons and *estanceiros* (ranch owners). Food was plentiful, except during droughts, but it was monotonous.

For most first-generation pioneers, home was little more than a shed, hastily assembled from whatever lay to hand – rough-hewn logs or sods hacked from the ground, with a floor of beaten earth and a thatched roof. Mud-coated walls were breeding grounds for bacteria and vermin. Accidents with tools, guns and horses, snake bites, epidemics, natural disasters, and the routine perils of childbirth, made sudden death an everyday occurrence. Standards of hygiene were low and professional medical assistance usually out of reach.

For the average pioneer, the harshness of the surroundings, coupled with isolation, loneliness and boredom, were more typical daily experiences than conviviality and stimulation. There was little to read – if one could read – and few beyond immediate family to talk to. Alcoholism was a common refuge for many. Mental, as much as physical, self-sufficiency was essential for survival.

The conditions of frontier living did little to foster culture, although heroic efforts were made, particularly by women, to preserve the little rituals and comforts of domestic life, such as a curtained window, a neatly made garment, or a patch of flowers outside a cabin door. Socialising was usually a by-product of worship; the observance of patriotic occasions; or the celebration of such agricultural or domestic tasks as raising the roof

ROMANCE AND REALITY Above: Artists often idealised native peoples, depicting them as living in harmony with undisturbed nature. Right: Brazilian Indians wear European dress; such clothing was often seen as the first step to civilisation.

ENGINEERING FEATS A Union Pacific locomotive pulls flat cars across 'Big Trestle' near Promontory, Utah, in 1869.

on a new barn or assembling a patchwork quilt. Diversions were simple – dancing, card-playing, horseracing, drinking and brawling.

LITERATURE AND LETTERS

Although few pioneers had the leisure or the learning for literature, their struggles and endurance inspired many to write down what they saw. Classic works flowed from the pens of those who grew up or passed among them. James Fenimore Cooper's *The Last of the Mohicans* (1826), was one of a series of adventure stories about the American Indians and British rule. A generation later, a single tragicomic short story, *The Luck of Roaring Camp* (1870), established Bret Harte as the chronicler of the mining frontier. It enabled him to found *The Overland Chronicle Monthly* in 1868, the first outlet for Jack London, who wrote *The Call of the Wild* (1903) and *White Fang* (1906), and who was destined to become the richest and most celebrated American author of his day. Canada's frontier bard, Robert Service, wrote popular verse, such as *The*

Shooting of Dan McGrew (1907). His Australian counterpart, Henry Lawson, also wrote popular verse and celebrated the cult of 'mateship' in a series of short stories, such as *While the Billy Boils* (1896). Ironically, the New Zealand writer Katherine Mansfield (1888-1923) only found fame after she emigrated to Europe in 1908, but her writing drew largely on her memories of an Antipodean childhood.

THE DREAM . . . AND THE REALITY

As individuals, pioneers were often humbled by their own ignorance; but as societies, they behaved with extreme arrogance. Europeans believed that land could not merely be seized and used, but that it could also be denied to others. Of all the white man's weapons, few were stranger than the fence, a device as incomprehensible to the Plains Indian as to the Australian Aborigine.

Pioneers drained swamps, felled forests and irrigated barren plains to bring millions of square miles of land into cultivation; they also introduced new crops and species of livestock. But sometimes they were guilty of plundering the land so carelessly that they destroyed entire species of wildlife.

In 1620, when the Pilgrim Fathers arrived in America, there was a population of nine billion passenger pigeons. Subsequently shot as food for hogs, they had become extinct by the end of the 19th century. The impact of European diseases on native peoples was even more catastrophic.

Native populations were also systematically exterminated, marginalised or exploited. In the United States, Argentina, South Africa and New Zealand, the contest between invader and defender was too fierce to be left to private initiatives; consequently, armies of regular troops employing the latest technologies of destruction were sent in by the colonising governments. Tribal divisions, inferior weapons, and vulnerability to disease and alcohol were also the enemies of native peoples.

The United States was the first settler nation to construct a transcontinental railroad, completed

FRONTIER SHOWMAN **Buffalo Bill's Wild West shows included cowboys, gauchos and vaqueros – and toured as successfully in Europe as they did in the USA.**

in 1869. This not only bound east to west, but also opened up 'the Great American Desert' to intensive cultivation, revolutionising global agriculture. Once meat and wheat could be brought from the Midwest to the east coast more cheaply than it could be taken halfway across Britain, British farmers had little option but to change what they grew and how they grew it. The Canadian transcontinental railway had just as much of an impact on Canadian commerce. The tracks of the iron horse also freed for trade the wool, mutton and gold of Australia and New Zealand, the coffee of Brazil, the flour and beef of Argentina, and the precious metals of South Africa.

FAITH AND HOPE **These Boer religious elders, like many pioneers, drew strength and authority from a literal interpretation of the Old Testament, believing themselves to be divinely inspired guides of a chosen people.**

THE AMERICAS: DESTINY'S HORIZON

America's boundless frontier offered promises of

freedom, wealth and adventure. But the redemption of these

promises exacted a high price in danger, disease, pain and sheer

backbreaking labour. Despite these privations, the pioneer family

portrayed above in 1850 all gaze with calm confidence towards

a brighter tomorrow.

PIONEER HUNTERS AND SETTLERS

Restless and hardy, but less concerned to tame the land than to survive it,

the first generations of mountain men served as unknowing

trailblazers for later settlers.

IN 1802 THE FRENCH traveller F.A. Marchaux journeyed from Ohio to Missouri to see for himself whether the frontier land was as fertile as reported and whether the country was truly overrun with beaver, bison and elk. The round trip involved a journey of some 1500 miles (2400 km). Marchaux thought the apparent restlessness of the settlers was irrational: 'It was they who began to clear . . . fertile countries, and wrested them from the savages . . . after five or six years' bloody war; but the long habit of wandering and idle life has prevented their enjoying the fruit of their labours, and profiting by the very price to which these lands have risen in so short a time.'

Visitors from conservative Europe saw in the frontiersman a lack of steadiness of purpose and dedication, an inability to follow a settled course of action. But the Americans themselves knew better. Christopher C. Andrews, a New Hampshire man who became a rich lumber merchant in Minnesota, recognised that frontier 'restlessness' was as deliberate as the schemes of any city slicker: '. . .the story of the pioneer who was disturbed by society

when his nearest neighbour lived 15 miles (24 km) off, even if it be true, fails to give the correct reason for the migratory life of this class of men'. The typical frontiersman was a solitary figure, dressed in a short jacket and baggy trousers. Around his waist he wore a sash, partly for swagger, partly to hold a huge knife, a tomahawk and a couple of beaver snares. Cradled in his arms he carried a long-barrelled rifle and draped over his shoulder a bright, striped blanket. Travelling alone by canoe and camping each night on the river bank, he would pause every few days to hunt. What he killed he ate, saving the hides and pelts to exchange for powder and shot.

The reason such men chose to live lonely, hard and dangerous lives was the prospect of profit. It drove the frontier forward and, when it was realised in abundance, drove it farther forward still. Americans were seldom willing to let what was good stand in the way of what was even better. As Andrews noted: 'The farmer of Ohio does not expect to find better soil than he leaves; but his inducements are that he can sell his land at $40 or $50 an acre, and pre-empt as good in Minnesota for a dollar and a quarter an acre. This operation leaves him a surplus fund, and he becomes a more opulent man, with

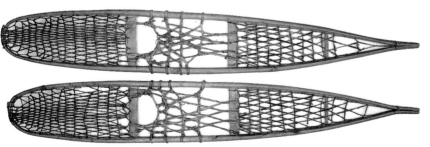

EQUIPPED FOR SURVIVAL
The hunter's metal bear trap and ash-framed snowshoes were essential tools of his trade. His homemade fur and buckskin clothing provided excellent camouflage and was durable, comfortable and easy to repair.

JOURNEY'S END?
Fur trappers take the opportunity to rest on the trail. Trappers, archetypal pioneers, had been plying their roving trade in North America since the 16th century.

better means to adorn his farm and to educate his children . . . when a man earns a few dollars he can easily invest it in a piece of land, and double his money in three months, perhaps in one month.'

THE SEQUENCE OF SETTLEMENT

Such a constantly moving population created a wave-like pattern of settlement, which transformed the land in a recognisable series of stages.

First came the hunters. They usually built nothing more permanent than a lean-to of brush and bark, supported on poles. At night they slept beneath it on the ground, rolled in a blanket, with a fire blazing on the open side to ward off animal predators and throw some light on human ones. Hunters lived off the game they shot or snared and supplemented their diet with wild fruits and berries. As

PELT TO FELT The 83-year-old survivor of many lonely winters (right) smokes contemplatively while dressing a beaver skin. Beaver fur produced a fine felt, lustrous and waterproof, which could be blocked to make imposing headgear for dandies, soldiers and even clerics, as shown below.

the game began to thin out, the hunters moved on. Apart from spreading a knowledge of the territory and acting as guides for permanent settlers, they left no mark of their passing.

Next came the backwoodsmen, who built crude cabins that were barely large enough to sleep in.

continued on page 18

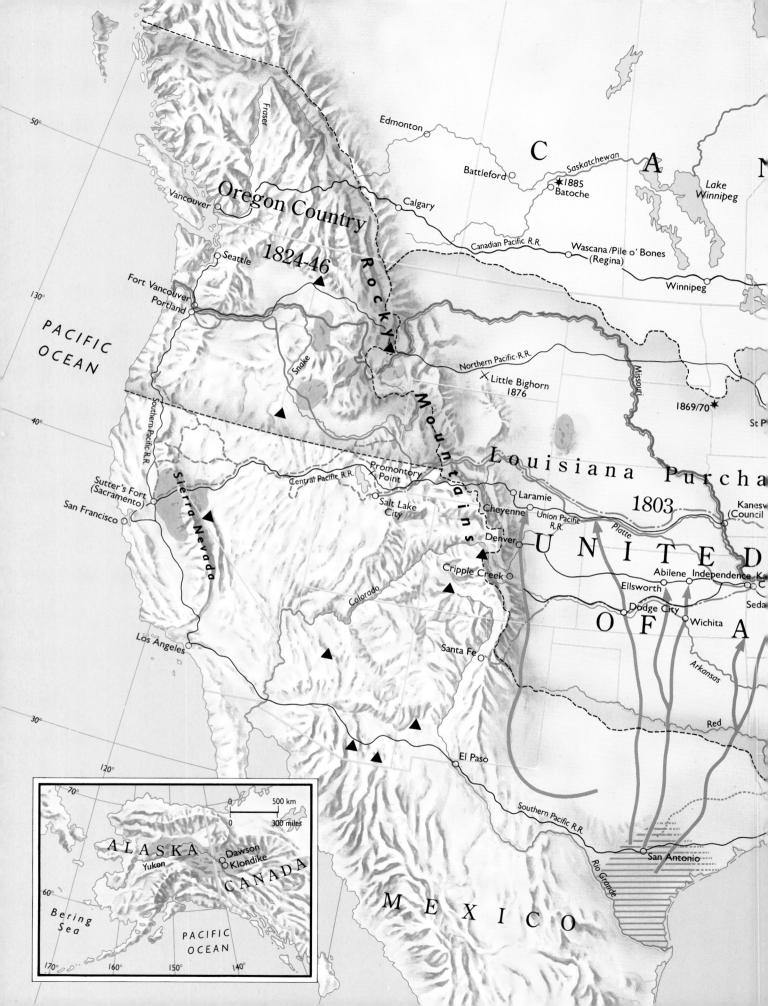

PACIFIC
OCEAN

50°

130°

40°

PACIFIC
OCEAN

120°

30°

Oregon Country

1824-46

Vancouver

Seattle

Fort Vancouver
Portland

Snake

Southern Pacific R.R.

Sierra Nevada

Sutter's Fort
(Sacramento)

San Francisco

Central Pacific R.R.

Promontory
Point

Salt Lake
City

Los Angeles

Colorado

Santa Fe

El Paso

Edmonton

Battleford

Calgary

C   A   N

Saskatchewan

★ 1885
Batoche

Lake
Winnipeg

Canadian Pacific R.R.

Wascana/Pile o' Bones
(Regina)

Winnipeg

Rocky

Mountains

Missouri

Northern Pacific R.R.

× Little Bighorn
1876

Louisiana Purcha

1803

1869/70 ★

St P

Laramie

Cheyenne

Denver

Union Pacific
R.R.

Platte

UNITED

Kanesw
(Council

Cripple Creek

Abilene   Independence   Ka

Ellsworth

Dodge City

O   F

Wichita

Seda

A

Arkansas

Red

Southern Pacific R.R.

Rio Grande

San Antonio

M   E   X   I   C   O

ALASKA

Yukon

Dawson
Klondike

CANADA

70°

60°

Bering
Sea

PACIFIC
OCEAN

170°   160°   150°   140°

500 km

0   300 miles

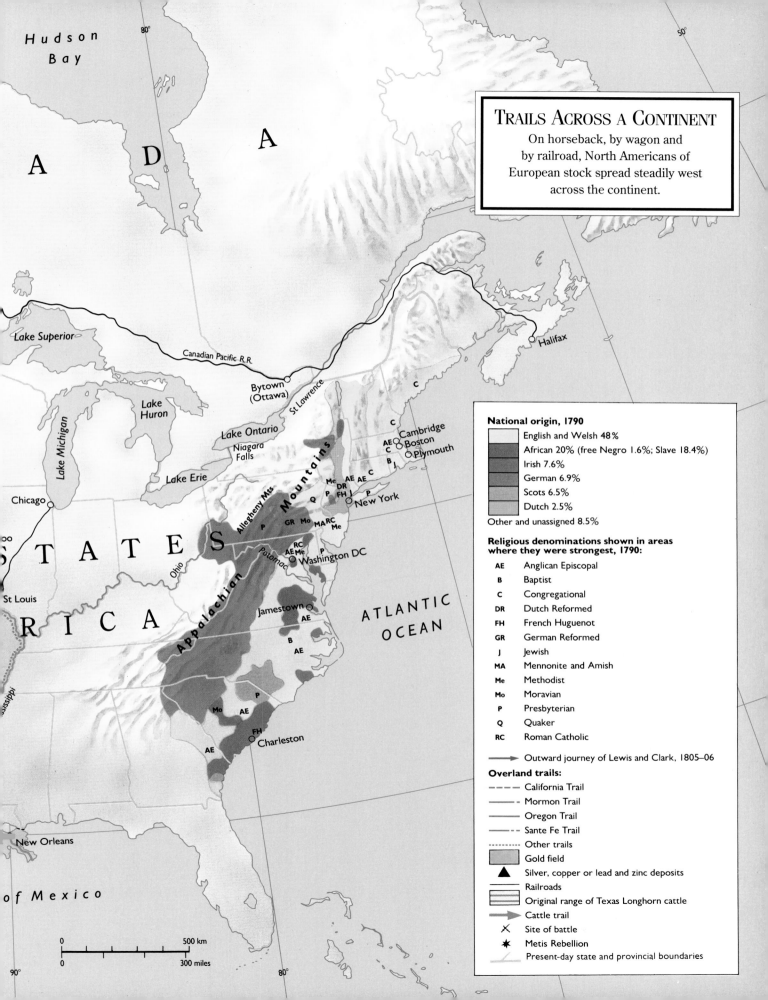

Hudson
Bay

A   D   A

Canadian Pacific R.R.

Lake Superior

Lake Huron

Lake Michigan

St Lawrence

Bytown
(Ottawa)

Halifax

C

Cambridge
Boston
Plymouth

Lake Ontario

Niagara
Falls

Lake Erie

Chicago

S T A T E S

St Louis

RICA

Mississippi

AE
B

C
AE AE

C

Me   AE
DR
Q   P FH J
GR Mo
MA RC
AE RC   Me
AEMe P
Washington DC

New York

Allegheny Mts

Mountains

Appalachian

Ohio

Potomac

Jamestown
AE

B
AE

P

Mo   AE

FH
AE   Charleston

ATLANTIC
OCEAN

New Orleans

of Mexico

TRAILS ACROSS A CONTINENT
On horseback, by wagon and
by railroad, North Americans of
European stock spread steadily west
across the continent.

National origin, 1790
English and Welsh 48%
African 20% (free Negro 1.6%; Slave 18.4%)
Irish 7.6%
German 6.9%
Scots 6.5%
Dutch 2.5%
Other and unassigned 8.5%

**Religious denominations shown in areas
where they were strongest, 1790:**

AE	Anglican Episcopal
B	Baptist
C	Congregational
DR	Dutch Reformed
FH	French Huguenot
GR	German Reformed
J	Jewish
MA	Mennonite and Amish
Me	Methodist
Mo	Moravian
P	Presbyterian
Q	Quaker
RC	Roman Catholic

→ Outward journey of Lewis and Clark, 1805–06

Overland trails:
- - - - - California Trail
———— Mormon Trail
———— Oregon Trail
— · — · Sante Fe Trail
· · · · · Other trails
▨ Gold field
▲ Silver, copper or lead and zinc deposits
════ Railroads
▨ Original range of Texas Longhorn cattle
⟹ Cattle trail
✕ Site of battle
✶ Metis Rebellion
       Present-day state and provincial boundaries

0   500 km
0   300 miles

CANADIAN TRADERS

Canadian fur trappers reached the Rockies by 1754 – two decades before American settlers had begun to advance into Kentucky. In 1763 British negotiators considered handing all 3 850 000 sq miles (9971 km²) of Canada back to France in return for the 687 sq mile (1780 km²) sugar-rich Caribbean island of Guadeloupe.

Two men could raise such a dwelling in less than three days. They would clear a patch of forest to plant corn but grew only what they needed to eat, rather than to raise a surplus for sale. Virgin soil was so fertile it would yield a ton and a half of corn per acre (0.4 ha). The English bluestocking Harriet Martineau was assured by a teasing Kentuckian that: 'If you plant a nail at night, 'twill come up a spike next morning.' Although thinking of some two or three hundred acres as 'their' land, even a large family might cultivate as little as eight or ten. Those fortunate enough to have maples nearby had a convenient source of syrup and sugar to flavour their food or use for barter. Wives and children gathered the fruits of the

GRISLY ENCOUNTER Mountain man S.E. Hollister (left) escaped from this encounter with only a badly mauled arm. Grizzlies averaged 8 ft (2.4 m) in height and weighed 800 lb (362 kg). Below: In the wilderness, rivers were vital to communication and the canoe was the ideal form of transportation.

THE TRAILBLAZERS – LEWIS AND CLARK

FRONTIERSMEN The scientific expedition led by Lewis and Clark brought back a wealth of data from North America's uncharted frontier regions. The serious expressions and elegant dress of their official portraits only hint at the steely toughness that bore them through their ordeal.

WHEN THOMAS JEFFERSON bought the vast Louisiana Territory from France sight unseen, Virginians Meriwether Lewis and William Clark undertook a three-year odyssey at his instruction to find out what sort of bargain he had got for the taxpayer. Backed by a team of 34 soldiers and ten civilians, whose skills ranged from map-making to medicine and from carpentry to Indian sign-language, they set off up the Missouri on May 14, 1804. Wintering in what became North Dakota, they met Toussaint Charbonneau, a French-Canadian fur trapper, and Sacagawea, his teenage Indian mistress; henceforth this couple served the expedition as guide and interpreter, Sacagawea bearing her baby, Jean-Baptiste, on her back for the next 4000 miles (6400 km). Having a woman among their number signalled to potential enemies that the expedition did not constitute a war-party, and not a single skirmish was fought throughout the entire journey. Sacagawea was invaluable as an interpreter and she also shared her knowledge of how to live off the land and helped her employers to negotiate for horses and guides. After a wretched second winter, passed on the Pacific coast, the expedition started back, reaching St Louis in March 1806. Only two men had been lost – one by desertion, the other from a burst appendix.

Peaceful contact had been established with at least six new tribes previously unknown in the East. A huge amount of data had been collected about the culture of native peoples, about the flora and fauna of the West and about the potential richness of 'Oregon' – an immense, fertile region beyond the Rockies – which simply cried out for settlers. Above all, the basic features of the geography of the western half of the continent had been established and accurately mapped.

In recognition of their services, Lewis and Clark were each granted 1600 acres (650 ha) of land. Their men were given 320 acres (130 ha) each, plus a bonus. Lewis, appointed Governor of Louisiana Territory, died soon afterwards. Clark, who adopted two of Sacagawea's children, became Governor of Missouri and Superintendent of Indian Affairs. Sacagawea's fate is disputed. She may have died of 'putrid fever' in her mid 20s or have returned to her own people, the Shoshone. And Toussaint Charbonneau went back to being a fur trapper.

DATABASE Clark's journal notes the dimensions of North America's largest bird, the Californian condor, identified by him as a 'large buzzard'.

TRADE GOODS Native American trapper families, such as this one (left), in their lodge near Fort Garry in the 1820s traded furs for European-style goods, such as clothes and household utensils. Below: The exchange value of this trade token, with George IV on the face and a beaver on the reverse, was one pelt.

forest – walnuts, berries, wild plums, grapes and crab apples. What was not immediately eaten was made into preserves to see them through the winter.

These first settlers were hunters rather than farmers. Their main quarry were deer, turkey and opossum but they also killed and ate elk, bear, raccoon, duck and squirrel. Bear meat was cured as a sort of bacon, rendering out the fat by boiling, then salting and smoking the residue. Bear oil was used as a substitute for butter or hog lard. Turkeys were preserved by salting, although salt was neither cheap nor easy to obtain.

Most backwoodsmen were squatters, with no legal title to the land they lived on. Nevertheless, most hoped to profit from the 'improvements' they had made by handing them over to a newcomer in return for a modest cash payment, and moving on westwards to do the same thing over again. In 1841 the United States Congress accepted that this was how the frontier land market actually worked and passed a general 'pre-emption law', which gave the occupant of a piece of land the right to

buy it at the minimum price set by government. The squatter could thus pre-empt the public auction, where it might fall into the hands of speculators or fraudsters – people who would do little or nothing towards the hard labour of actual settlement, but looked to make their fortunes through buying, selling or deception. The true settler cleared more land each year, fencing it to establish what could properly be called, and recognised as, a farm. Between 1830 and 1850 in the region north of the Ohio and the Missouri, an average of 20 000 new farms were established each summer. Between 1840 and 1850 the population nearly doubled in both Mississippi and Missouri. In Wisconsin during the same decade it grew tenfold.

MAKING A HOME

In time the settled farmer built a bigger, better cabin, using existing buildings as outhouses for storage, workshops or stabling. Cabins were built of tree trunks, notched to fit together. Initially, a cabin consisted of a single room up to 30 ft (9 m) long and about half as wide. In French Canada the

LOG-CABIN IDYLL In this idealised scene of contentment, a group of trappers survey their boat of pelts while supper cooks over an open fire. The reality of wilderness living was very much tougher.

earliest cabins were built of posts driven into the ground, rather than a series of logs laid horizontally on top of each other. A more sophisticated, later version used a framework of upright posts grooved to receive stable, short, squared-off horizontals. As the bottom layer rotted, it could be kicked out and an additional slat added to the top. Americans preferred the 'Pennsylvanian' style of house construction, which had shaped, interlocking tree trunks at the corners. This building technique had originated among Swedish-Finnish colonists who lived along the Delaware River in the 17th century. The chinks between the logs

TAKE YOUR PARTNERS! A frontier fiddler squats on a barrel, sawn in half to make a stool. The violin, like the mouth organ, was a universal accompaniment to songs and dances.

were packed with mud or moss to keep out the wind. Later on, the interior walls might be plastered with mud and whitewashed or lined with sawn boards.

In the absence of any other form of heating, fireplaces were generously large, often stretching the full width of the cabin. In summer, womenfolk usually cooked outdoors to minimise smoke, heat and the risk of fire. Early settlers, fearful of Indian attack, sometimes limited their cabins to a single, narrow door, dispensing altogether with windows. In more settled areas, there was usually a door on each side of the house to help to evacuate smoke, with a small window cut through the log wall to admit light and air.

As glass for windows was both scarce and expensive, old newspapers greased with hog's lard were often used as a substitute. During the enforced idleness of winter, the settler might board over the dirt floor, perhaps leaving a space between it and the ground to use for storage or the safekeeping of valuables. Another sophistication would have been a loft, reached by a ladder. This also served as a storeroom and bedroom, allowing parents to separate themselves from their children or

provide a bed for the night for visitors. The mattresses they used were either stuffed with dried leaves or, along the lower reaches of the Mississippi, dried Spanish moss. The availability of feather-bedded mattresses depended upon the growth of flocks of ducks and chickens, or the collection of plumage from game birds.

Furnishings were minimal and consisted of open shelves, pegs and poles, on which clothes and household items were ranged. Prize possessions would certainly have included a rifle, an axe, possibly a scythe and a few pewter mugs, plates or bowls. Utensils bought from stores consisted of a frying pan, cooking pots and a kettle, and perhaps a griddle or even a spit; but, when it came to tableware, homemade wooden bowls and trenchers were more common than earthenware crocks.

TAMING TALL TIMBERS The two-handed saw, like the heavy axe, was another product of the industrial East that played an essential part in the opening up of the wild Western frontier.

SETTLING IN As time went by, the early settlers managed to achieve a level of comfort that they had known in the Old World, as seen in this picture of a New England home.

Containers of all kinds were quite scarce. Emigrants from Europe were advised to seal possessions not needed on their journey in a barrel; this not only protected them from damage and pilferage but also provided an invaluable holdall on arrival. Catherine Traill, who emigrated to Ontario in 1832, advised readers of her *Female Emigrant's Guide* to make chairs by sawing a barrel in half. Skilled coopers (barrel-makers) were in short supply on the frontier, and many settlers had to use roughly hollowed tree trunks for storage purposes instead. Some imitated native skills and learned to weave lightweight boxes from the bark of hickory or elm trees. Wood cleared from the land was rough-hewn into tables, benches and stools; chairs were more difficult to make and less suited to uneven floors.

As prosperity increased, rooms could quite easily be added on to the existing house by cutting a hole through the log wall to serve as an inner doorway to the extra rooms, which would then be built on, as and when needed. In the warmer, southern climes a porch or verandah might be built right round the house to provide much-needed shade throughout the day. When a sawmill was set up in an area, the better-off would be able to move into a timber-framed house clad with evenly sawn 'clapboarding' from the mill.

CLEARINGS AND CROPS

The settlers were prepared to endure such difficult living conditions because they had come here specifically to cultivate the land. However, clearing forest cover to create plots of land for agriculture entailed felling every tree individually.

The first crop a family grew was generally corn (maize). Unlike wheat, corn could be planted and harvested satisfactorily – even on land littered with stumps and roots. Corn was the staple of the frontier diet, eaten by humans and livestock alike. F.A. Marchaux noted that: '. . . they make loaves of it from eight to ten pounds, which they bake in ovens, or small cakes baked on a board before the fire. This bread is generally eaten hot, and is not very palatable to those who are not used to it'. The main drawback with corn was that squirrels and crows also liked it. Scaring them off by shouting and banging pans was a regular summer occupation for generations of small boys who knew that, once harvested, the corn would be turned into the 'johnnycakes' they ate as snacks, and the 'mush and milk' served at breakfast. Alongside the corn, the farmer cleared a patch for turnips. These provided winter fodder for livestock and 'tops' which the family would eat as 'greens', just as they did

THE GREAT OUTDOORS Settlers carried out a wide range of daily tasks. In the harsh winter, milking or chopping wood might be carried out in the barn.

THE FATE OF A FRONTIER FAMILY

BETWEEN 1810 and 1814 the lawyer and author Henry M. Brackenridge (1786-1871) lived in the newly acquired Territory of Louisiana. Travelling through the future state of Missouri, he met a family of newcomers – a husband, his wife and their 14 children. Originally from Connecticut, the family had hoped to settle in Ohio, but they had found the land there already too dear, and had pushed onwards to the 'extreme frontier':

❝ I drew near a settler's cabin, and discovered a group of persons seated by a large fire . . . They were

all glowing with health . . . neatly dressed in new cotton cloth and had nothing of that wretchedness or poverty, or stupid ignorance, which is but too common in the unfortunate peasantry of most countries . . . We all entered the cabin, where the table was spread, and rough benches placed around it. A tin cup filled with rich milk was placed before each of us and cakes of the Indian meal were smoking on the board. The good man said grace in a reverend manner and we did ample justice to the simple and wholesome fare provided for us . . .

Surrounded by health, innocence and benevolence, who could complain? After supper, we returned to the fire underneath the spreading tree, and whiled away the time in sprightly and mirthful conversation; the Yankee girls were very talkative, the whole family appeared to be delighted with our company in this lonely place, where

SURVIVAL **The frontier family faced deprivation and hardship as they tried to carve out a new life. Here settlers are reduced to a daily ration of five kernels of corn each.**

they so seldom saw any strangers but their neighbours, the bears and wolves . . . We again entered the house, where they sung one of Watts' pious hymns, after which our host poured out a prayer that seemed to flow from the very bottom of his heart . . . We were shown up to the loft, to which we ascended by a ladder. A few blankets and bear skins had been provided for us; we resigned ourselves to sleep, in the consciousness that even such wretches as we could not fail of experiencing the care of the protecting angel, set to guard this charming family.

. . . The autumn following I . . . anticipated much pleasure in seeing these worthy people. But alas! as I drew near the house, every thing appeared still about it, and, on my making a noise, the good man, emaciated to a skeleton, crawled out, and after recognising, informed me in the most pathetic, yet composed, manner of a train of misfortunes which had befallen him. His whole family had been assailed by violent, bilious fevers, his wife and five of his children were no more, and the rest, with the exception of two boys, who were then extremely ill, had been kindly taken away by some of the old settlers, that they might be the better attended to; but, said he, "God's will be done – it is all for the best". I could have wept . . . ❞

with the nettle tops, purslane and celandine that they gathered from uncleared land. Potatoes, dry peas and beans were good crops for winter storage and pumpkins were made into pies, the surplus juice being boiled down to convert it into a sort of molasses. When grain ran short, pumpkin or

ground, dried beans were added to the flour in order to stretch it.

Farmers eager to generate a cash crop opted for wheat or flax in the North and tobacco or cotton in the South. Once planted, orchards took time to bear fruit, so the peach tree became widely planted, not only because it yielded produce by the second year, but because its crop could be turned into a fierce brandy which, with apple cider, was the regular standby of homespun hospitality.

Hogs were the easiest livestock to raise, and pork became the staple meat of settled areas as the game gave out. Hogs ate the surplus of the corn harvest and other crops, and grubbed for themselves on uncleared land. Only in the harshest weather did they need to eat household waste as a supplement to their diet of acorns, roots and windfall fruits. The farmer killed off the weaker beasts at the onset of winter, his wife preserving their flesh and innards as bacon or sausages. Their fat was used for deep-frying doughnuts or crullers – a kind of cake made from a dough of flour, eggs and sugar fried in oil.

One of the biggest problems the earliest settlers faced was a shortage of mills for grinding corn or wheat. Many settlers devised their own methods of milling when faced with a mill owner's demand that they hand over half their crop in payment for grinding the other half. Water mills were common where streams flowed fast enough to drive them, but they could be immobilised by frost or drought. Some of the most effective were 'floating mills', supported on boats to take advantage of a river current. These were less vulnerable to attack by Native Americans and could be moved if the river dried up.

MAKING THE MOST OF IT Pigs were fed kitchen waste and corn husks in severe winters to yield useful meat, lard and hide, while the turkey (right) provided food as well as feathers for decorating clothes or for stuffing pillows and coverlets.

Rivers not only provided power but also served as the highways of frontier trade for decades before there were passable, all-weather roads. Marchaux noted that: 'This commerce consists [of] . . . hams and salted pork, brandies distilled from corn and peaches, butter, hemp, skins and various sorts of flour . . . Tradespeople who . . . go up and down the river in a canoe convey . . . haberdashery goods and more especially tea and coffee.'

DRINKING HABITS
Those who could not afford tea drank infusions of herbs such as sage or sassafras. By boiling parched corn with water, they could make a drink that the generous-minded referred to as 'coffee'. Another desperate

SWEET TALKING
Boiling up a batch of maple syrup provided the occasion for a good, long gossip with neighbours. Children were clearly expected to lend a hand.

25

expedient, misleadingly referred to as a 'beverage', was creek water flavoured with brown sugar and vinegar.

Most Americans lubricated their daily lives with strong drink. Drinking on the frontier was heroic in scale: peach brandy and corn whiskey were the standard tipples, mixed with sugar and water to make a toddy on special occasions. Every social gathering, however mundane, justified a copious consumption of alcohol; not just weddings, but also funerals, house-building, barn-raising, quilting, harvesting and husking.

Water was distrusted – often rightly. A traveller along the Ohio in 1807 found the river thick and turbid, and complained that 'the thousands of dead squirrels putrefying on its surface and its shores, contribute very little to render it . . . agreeable'. Strong liquor also played a central role in the fur trade, which was the lifeblood of the Canadian North-west. Canny Scots buyers entertained native hunters with round-the-clock, nonstop drinking bouts before their annual trading sessions, and concluded them in the same way.

Rainwater was much prized, both for its purity and because it did not have to be hauled up to the cabin a bucket at a time. The provident housewife put a trough or barrel outside her door to collect water coming off the roof. In times of drought, she would line up every available container to catch the occasional shower.

DRESSING THE PART

Pioneers not only built their own homes and grew their own food but, to a large extent, made their own clothes. The earliest settlers made much use of deerskin, though only among the poorest was it worn by women. The main garment was a long, baggy shirt, often rubbed with deer fat or bear grease to waterproof it. Fringes were not merely decorative but helped it to shed water faster; they could also be torn off to make running repairs to seams if they split.

Even when men wore pantaloons of coarse linen, they often protected their lower limbs with buckskin leggings. Moccasins were worn with dry oak leaves or moss in place of stockings. Such a costume served the hunter as ready-made camouflage, as well as being both comfortable and hard-wearing. Womenfolk spun and wove home-grown flax to make linen for shirts and skirts, and dyed it with the inner bark of the white walnut to give it a yellow-

FIREWATER Water was often dangerous to drink but alcohol, sometimes mixed with herbs, was drunk in copious amounts.

PUTTING A PUNCH IN IT Colonel Spangler's recipe for 'Cherry Bounce' suggests an ingenious method for using up surplus fruit and for taking some of the raw edge off homemade spirits.

THE ENGLISH FIND THEMSELVES TOLERATED BY THEIR HOST

MORRIS BIRKBECK, an Englishman who settled successfully in Illinois, found the journey westwards a democratising experience:

❛ In your reception at a western Pennsylvania tavern there is something of hospitality combined with the mercantile feelings of your host. He is generally a man of property, the head man of the village perhaps, with the title of Colonel, and feels that he confers, rather than receives, a favour by the accommodation he affords; and, rude as his establishment may be, he does not perceive that you have a right to complain: what he has you partake of, but he makes no apologies; and if you show symptoms of dissatisfaction or disgust, you will fare the worse; whilst a disposition to be pleased and satisfied will be met by a wish to make you so.

At the last stage, our party of eight weary pilgrims, dropping in as the evening closed, alarmed the landlady, who asked the ladies if we were not English, and said she would rather not wait upon us — we should be "difficult". However, she admitted us, and this morning, at parting, she said she liked to wait on "such" English; and begged we would write to our friends and recommend her house. We were often told that we were not "difficult", like the English; and I am sure our entertainment was the better, because they found us easy to please. ❜

HOME COMFORTS A neat picket fence protects the vegetable patch of this 1880s Idaho family from stray animals. The sturdy wheelbarrow (below) was an essential tool for settlers.

brown hue known as 'butternut'. Dresses or jackets made from 'boughten' calico or fustian – a tough linen-cotton mixture – might be kept for Sunday wear. The fastidious walked to the meeting house barefoot, carrying their shoes and stockings to save them from dirt and damage.

THE COLD COMFORTS OF FREEDOM
Male emigrants to 'Upper' (English-speaking) Canada in the 1830s were advised to protect themselves from the extreme cold and to be sure to bring a fur cap, a warm great coat, a thick woollen jacket, 'frocks' (overalls) of duck, canvas and jersey, four pairs of trousers, four shirts and four pairs of stockings. A warm cloak was advisable for the women.

Although most early frontier settlers found life hard, the land was fertile and belonged to them – and not a landlord to whom they would have to pay rent. Furthermore, taxes were very light, compared to the heavy taxation that they had experienced in the Old World. As a result, many settlers felt they had shaken themselves free from a restrictive and oppressive society. On the frontier, how a man and his family lived, ate and dressed depended much more on what they could do than on what they could buy. The tasks that faced them required energy, rather than expertise, and ingenuity rather than inspiration. Optimism was the American creed and the frontier was its natural breeding-ground.

THE FAR WEST AND THE PLAINS

The endless prairies of the West presented pioneers with an entirely different challenge from

the dense forests of the East. Their conquest of these arid and treeless lands demanded new tactics

and technologies. The axe gave way to barbed wire and the wind pump.

THE FIRST WHITE explorers of the arid and treeless region between the Mississippi and the Rockies dubbed the area 'the Great American Desert'. This was wildly misleading, for it was eventually to become not only America's breadbasket, but one of the most productive areas of the world. Ranging from up-state New York right down to Kentucky and Tennessee, the area posed settlement problems even more heartbreaking than those faced by the first generations of pioneers, who had carved out their farms from a thickly wooded, well-watered land abounding in game on the eastern coast of the continent. Farther west on the prairie, they had to build homes without lumber, burn fires without kindling, and grow crops virtually without rain on soil so matted and compressed that an ordinary plough could scarcely scratch its surface.

A NATION ENLARGED

As late as 1840, less than half the land west of the Mississippi was actually part of the territory of the United States. A vast portion of the Great Plains

MOBILE LIVING With the introduction of the horse from Europe in the 16th century, Native Americans were able to develop a new way of life on the plains – based on the hunting of bison, as shown in this painting of the 1850s.

THE DEATH OF THE BUFFALO — DEATH OF A CULTURE

SLAYING THE NOBLE BEAST Buffalo hides were shipped east to keep fashionable city dwellers warm in their winter sledges. Apart from cutting out the tongue, as shown above, the rest of the meat was left to rot.

IN 1893, the journalist Hamlin Russell chronicled the final demise of the buffalo for readers of *Harper's New Monthly Magazine*:
❛ The Union Pacific Railroad was completed in 1869 . . . and from that hour the fate of the buffalo was sealed . . . The animals seem to have divided into two great herds . . . The Southern herd was the first to go. Buffalo Bill and his kind, with English "sportsmen" and American army officers, vied with each other in the wanton slaughter . . . at the close of 1874 the great Southern herd was extinct.

In the North the conditions were more favourable but the relentless hunter was hot upon the trail of the diminishing herds. In 1876 Fort Benton alone sent eighty thousand hides to market. In 1883 two carloads of hides were shipped from

OLD BONES Although buffalo meat was rejected, their bones found a market as an industrial raw material or were ground up and used as fertiliser.

Dickinson, North Dakota . . . This was the last year of the Buffalo – 1883. I remember seeing on the plains a great stack of whitening bones . . . This is all that is left of the buffalo now out of which the Indian can find profit. Once he obtained [from buffalo] food, clothing, building material for his tepees, bones from which he could fashion weapons, and hides which he could sell or use in the making of canoes . . . Now the Eastern sugar refineries purchase the bones . . . to be used in clarifying sugar. . . .

As long as the buffalo roamed through the Indian country, the settlement of the land and the extinction of the Indian title was practically an impossibility. With his food supply cut off, the Indian became suddenly tame and easy to handle. ❜

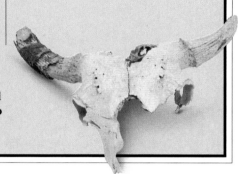

had been acquired by the purchase of the Louisiana Territory from the French in 1803, but even 40 years later few Americans actually lived there, and it remained almost entirely the unchallenged hunting ground of nomadic Native Americans. At the southern extremity of the plains lay Texas, a province of Mexico until it revolted successfully in 1835-6 and joined the USA a decade later. The land west of Texas, which was inhabited by Mexican ranchers, American fur traders and native peoples who lived by a combination of hunting and farming, also belonged to Mexico, until it was annexed by war in 1846-8. To the north-west lay the 'Oregon Country' – an area much larger than the future state of Oregon – jointly claimed by Britain and America, though sparsely settled.

The first parts of the West to attract large numbers of American settlers were the 'fertile fringes' – Texas, Oregon and California. The river valleys of southern Texas could be cultivated in much the same way as farms in Missouri, Kentucky and Tennessee, where many sold out or abandoned their existing holdings. The white population of Texas rose from 30 000 at the time of its Independence to 150 000 by the mid 19th century. In 1840 all the Americans in Oregon – less than 150 in total – would scarcely have filled a decent-sized chapel. In 1843 the first wagon train blazed an

HISPANIC HORIZONS Founded during 1609-10, Santa Fe became the capital of New Mexico in 1851.

'Oregon Trail' of 2000 miles (3200 km) to cross the Great Plains and the Rockies and reach the Columbia River. 'Oregon Fever' then drew so many from the east that by 1845 the 6000 Americans living there so far outnumbered the 750 British that the British government ceded all lands south of the 49th parallel to US sovereignty. California, when it was annexed from Mexico in 1848, had a population of 14 000. The discovery of gold in 1848 raised its population to 250 000 barely four years later. Further discoveries of gold, silver, lead and copper from the Canadian border to Colorado kept the adventurous pouring westwards.

FITTING OUT

The usual starting points for crossing the prairie were Council Bluffs in Iowa, St Joseph in Missouri and, most favoured of all, the aptly named Independence in Missouri, the adopted home of Tennessee-born trader Josiah Gregg (1806-50). Gregg wrote an account, published in 1844, of the business conducted along the Santa Fe Trail, a wagon route from Missouri to Santa Fe, the capital of New Mexico. In *The Commerce of the Prairies*, he emphasised the town's ideal location as a jumping-off point, barely more

DECLARATION OF INDEPENDENCE Wagons pass the courthouse at Independence, Missouri, at the beginning of their long and arduous trek to freedom in the West.

than 3 miles (5 km) off the Missouri River and only 12 miles (20 km) from the border with Indian territory. Would-be settlers could travel thus far, encumbered only by their household possessions and, on the very brink of their great odyssey, equip themselves with the bulky provisions and transport they would need to see them across to the promised land. Gregg reckoned that every adult male needed to lay in 50 lb (23 kg) each of flour and bacon, 20 lb (9 kg) of sugar and 10 lb (4.5 kg) of coffee as a basic diet. Bacon would keep as long as it was protected from direct heat; packing it in a barrel of bran usually afforded sufficient insulation. Beans and crackers he regarded as 'dispensable luxuries'. The bulk of the traveller's diet would be supplied by buffalo, antelope or rabbit shot along the way; but later emigrants would have to rely much more on their own cattle.

MOVING THE CAPITAL

It was proposed in 1870 that the federal capital of the US should be shifted from Washington to St Louis, Missouri, to reflect the westward shift in the population. At that time Missouri was the fourth most populous state in the Union.

As for transport, most used a wagon, usually drawn by a team of eight oxen or mules. Larger wagons, capable of hauling a load of 5000 lb (2 tonnes), were also available but these needed teams of 10 or 12. Oxen were only just over half the price of mules, stronger in muddy or sandy places, far more docile, less inclined to stray, and capable of grazing off virtually anything. But, as the prairie grass became shorter and drier, they often lost their strength and would 'arrive at their destination

continued on page 34

GO WEST, YOUNG MAN! After the Civil War, Kansas was promoted as a desirable destination for freed slaves from the South. An emigrant handbook of 1869 (far left) painted an optimistic picture.
Below: Pioneers pose for a picture; usually, however, only the sick or feeble would travel in the wagon.

THE WAGON TRAIN

WHEN THE wagon train halted for the evening, the women began cooking, the children were sent off to gather 'buffalo chips' of dried dung to feed the campfires and the men busied themselves with running repairs to their vehicles or, while the light lasted, hunted birds or small game for the pot.

The orderly circling of wagons each night gave their occupants both practical and psychological security. Regular routines not only ensured efficient progress but maintained morale and, at a deeper level, symbolised the pioneers' determination to carry the patterns of 'civilised' life with them into the lawless wilderness.

in a most shocking plight', suffering from tender feet. Some owners 'shoed' them with moccasins made of raw buffalo skins; these lasted well enough in dry weather but soon wore through in the wet.

Only families with substantial capital could contemplate the expenditure involved in crossing the continent. Compared with a labourer who might earn 50¢ a day, plus his food, and a skilled man who might earn up to $5 a day, a wagon and oxen cost at least $400 and food and utensils another $140. On top of this came tools, bedding and suitable clothing. The minimum needed was about $700, although some large families spent double that. Most raised the money by selling an existing farm.

Four out of five who undertook the trek had already moved at least once in search of a better life. In virtually every documented case it was the husband, not the wife, who opted to move; women were invariably reluctant to part from the network of relatives, neighbours and friends which provided mutual support in times of poverty, pregnancy or sickness. Almost half of all pioneers went as extended families, including

not only parents but also grandparents, adult offspring and their spouses. About a third of all single men attached themselves to family groups. They were glad to be fed and have their mending done, while the families were glad of another gun and pair of hands to protect their stock and work their land when they eventually reached it.

THE WAGON TRAIN

A train of 40 wagons would be formed at a starting point under a raid captain (usually an ex-military man), whose orders they bound themselves to obey. The train would stretch for over half a mile (1 km) and be on the move for over 12 hours a day, covering on average perhaps just over 1 mile (1.6 km) an hour. Only infants, the sick and the feeble rode; everyone else walked in order to spare the draught animals. Wagons jolted so much that surplus milk, in pails hung beneath them, would be churned to butter in the course of a single day's march. The journey to Oregon usually took eight months; even so, the schedule was tight. Going too early in April meant there would not be enough grass to graze the livestock; going too late could mean getting caught by snow in the coastal mountains.

Along the way, there was a strict sexual division of labour. Men drove and repaired wagons, looked after the livestock, stood guard and hunted. Women got up half an hour before their menfolk to gather fuel, start fires and milk cows. Preparing food was a daily trial; as one emigrant observed tartly, 'them that eat the most breakfast eat the most sand'. Apart from cooking, making beds, washing and mending clothes and controlling children, women were also expected to care for the sick and injured. At least 20 000 – roughly one out of

LIFE ON THE TRAIL The risk of disease (far right) was ever present. Self-medication such as quinine (right) was often the only treatment available. Below: Small parties of stragglers offered an easy target to Indians, who rarely attacked the well-organised wagon trains.

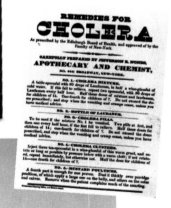

RECORDER OF A RAPIDLY DISAPPEARING WORLD

GEORGE CATLIN (1796-1872) abandoned a successful career as a society portrait painter in Philadelphia to travel the Great Plains from 1832 to 1837, and from 1852 to 1857, chronicling the disappearing way of life of 48 different tribes in 600 pictures and three major books. Catlin respected Native Americans and won their respect in return, and recorded both what he admired and what he could not but condemn:

❧ Amongst their feats of riding, there is one that has astonished me more than anything of the kind I have ever seen . . . a stratagem of war, learned and practised by every young man in the tribe; by which he was liable to drop his body upon the side of his horse at the instant

FRONTIER ART **This portrait of the artist Catlin dates from 1849. Below: Catlin was astonished by the equestrian skills of Plains Indians such as the Comanches. His paintings often emphasised the dignity of America's native people.**

he is passing, effectually screened from his enemies' weapons as he lays in a horizontal position behind the body of his horse, with his heel hanging over the horse's back; by which he has the power of throwing himself up again, and changing to the other side of the horse if necessary. In this wonderful condition he will hang whilst his horse is at fullest speed, carrying with him his bow and his shield, and also his long lance of 14 ft (4.2 m), all or either of which he will wield upon his enemy as he passes; rising and throwing his arrows over the horse's back or with equal ease and success under the horse's neck.

The tribe was going where hunger and dire necessity compelled them to go, and this pitiable object, who had once been a chief . . . who was now too old to travel, being reduced to mere skin and bones, was to be left to starve or meet with such death as might fall to his lot, and his bones to be picked by the wolves! . . . He said: "My children, our nation is poor, and it is necessary that you should all go to the country where you can get meat – my eyes are dimmed and my strength is no more; my days are nearly numbered, and I am a burthen to my children – I cannot go and I wish to die. Keep your hearts stout, and think not of me; I am no longer good for anything." ❧

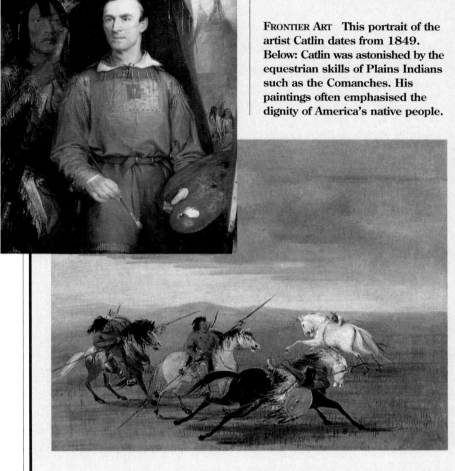

every 17 who started the journey – were buried along the overland trails, far more dying from disease or accident than by hostile action. Cholera was the biggest killer. A full-size wagon train was a formidable target for a band of Indians to raid, especially when it was corralled into a defensive circle, each wagon chained to its neighbour. It was the solitary wagon or the straggler that ran a real risk of being attacked. The Indians' deadliest tactic was not direct assault but the prairie fire, started deliberately to panic livestock into stampeding so that they could be rounded up at leisure. Most

Native Americans, however, were more interested in trading with, or begging from, the transients, rather than in attacking them.

At the end of the journey lay a lifetime of hard work. All they had to live off, and work with, was what they had brought with them. Tools and heavy equipment, such as anvils, were in desperately short supply. So was cloth; many had to cut up wagon covers to make topcoats, lining them with animal pelts for warmth. Medicines were likewise improvised. They made eyewash from gunpowder dissolved in water, and cough syrup from onions mashed in sugar. Animal grease and turpentine became a universal salve. Mixed with lavender, the same compound served as a pomade to smear down unruly locks. As one newcomer observed

HOLDING THE LINE   In 1849 the US government bought a Wyoming trading post to establish a military presence along the Oregon Trail. Renamed Fort Laramie, it served as the main centre for relations with the Sioux. Below: Geronimo poses with his band of fearless Chiracahua Apache renegades in 1886.

ironically: 'I never saw so fine a population as in Oregon. They were honest, because there was nothing to steal; sober, because there was no liquor; there were no misers, because there was no money; they were industrious, because it was work or starve.'

THE WINTER WARS

After 1854, treaties of sale with native peoples opened Kansas and Nebraska to white settlement. Traditionally, Native Americans had no concept that land could be owned. Instead, they claimed rights of use. However, the Homestead Act of 1862 finally granted common folk what they had yearned for throughout most of a century – land, not at the low, controlled price of $1.25 an acre, but 160 acres (65 ha) *free*, to be held outright after five years of cultivation. By 1890, approximately 400 000 families had taken advantage of this legislation to start a farm; two-thirds failed. Many thousands could subscribe to the slogan chalked on the wagon of one ruined family: 'In God we trusted, in Kansas we busted.' As the newcomers moved in, the original inhabitants of the land were moved aside.

The US government estimated that there were 300 000 Plains Indians, divided into over 120 tribal groupings. In the decade after the end of the Civil War in 1865, the army fought over 200 battles and skirmishes, which effectively broke the resistance of the Native Americans, forcing them out of their traditional hunting grounds and onto official reservations. By 1890 the Native American population had reached an all-time low of 250 000. The massacre of Custer's entire command at the Battle of

GENERAL CUSTER The flamboyant George Armstrong Custer was only 37 years of age at the time of his death in the Battle of Little Big Horn, fought in 1876.

Little Big Horn in 1876 was the last major counterstroke to succeed, and on a quite exceptional scale.

The architect of white victory was the son of an Irish immigrant, with a well-deserved reputation for daring and ruthlessness and a less celebrated, but equally useful, appreciation of the vital importance of logistics. The Civil War confirmed both General Philip Sheridan's status as a national hero, and his own conviction that no enemy could long sustain the will to fight when deprived of the means to fight. This was achieved by burning tepees to deprive the Native Americans of shelter and killing their ponies so that they could not hunt or migrate. Sheridan, who had served in the Far West in his youth, had an abstract sympathy for the plight of his enemy: 'We took away their country, broke up their mode of living, their habits of life, introduced disease and decay among them, and it was for this and against this that they made war. Could anyone expect less?'

The general's understanding did nothing to take the edge off his pitiless strategy. Comfortably based in Chicago, the unkempt, foul-mouthed, pleasure-loving veteran had at his disposal only 18 000 men, scattered over 76 posts and camps, with which to impose his authority on a million square miles (2 600 000 sq km) of territory. Realising the utter futility of trying to pin down roaming war parties, Sheridan proposed to take the war to his enemies by striking at their villages

A US CAVALRYMAN ON GUARD DUTY

SERGEANT CALLAGHAN is the first to be woken by the last shift of the overnight guard. Today his task is to escort a small supply train from the railhead back to camp. He knows that this routine task can be more risky than a so-called campaign against marauding hostiles. Back in October 1868, he accompanied the 19th Kansas Volunteer Cavalry on the trail of a war party. They stuck to it until the following April and never even saw them.

Native Americans had more sense than to attack forts or large bodies of alert troops with fresh supplies. What they liked was to pick off isolated details, such as telegraph-wiring or timber-cutting parties, or to ambush targets which followed predictable routes through difficult country – like his own.

Stirring his men into life, Callaghan reflected how almost half of these 'American' soldiers had in fact been born elsewhere. The biggest contingent were, like himself, Irish, and the next, German-speaking. Many of them had served in the armies of their native countries, which was just as well, because it was only the exceptional commander who actually organised proper training to make sure that his men could ride or even shoot. The next largest group were Italians, who joined to learn English and because $13 a month was better than what they would get as day-labourers. Of the native-born Americans many were Civil War veterans who knew no other trade but fighting. Others were drunks or men on the run from their debts, their families or the law. The steadier ones had been farmers or teamsters. Others claimed to have been craftsmen or storekeepers, and there were even a few self-styled 'attorneys' and 'professors'. The average age of first-time recruits was in the early 20s, with re-enlisting men a decade older. A third of the recruits would desert; some were 'snowbirds' who joined up to be fed through the winter then, when the snows melted, they melted away too, taking their rifle, saddle and horse. It was ironic that the best-disciplined and most loyal troopers were the free blacks of the 9th and 10th Cavalry – who had no prospect of promotion to officer rank.

Breakfast in the camp consisted of hardtack biscuits, salt pork and coffee. The beans were green, and had to be roasted and then pounded with a pistol butt before they could be used. The older hands added onions or potatoes to their food. These personal supplies, like the big Sheffield-made 'Bowie' knives that they used to chop firewood, open cans or skin game, were bought at their own expense.

Once the detail was on the move, Callaghan rode up and down the line, cajoling and commending. He knew that his men were anything but smart. Many had abandoned the uniform hat in favour of more practical broad-brimmed ones of felt or straw. Most wore 'store-bought' shirts which were better quality than standard-issue ones. Their uniform pants of rough 'kersey' were often reinforced in the seat with patches cut from flour sacks. As the fort finally came into sight, Callaghan summoned his men to a passable level of soldierly smartness. The prospect of beer and hard liquor did as much for their obedience as for their morale.

AT EASE A typical scene of daily life for the cavalrymen is portrayed in *A Cavalryman's Breakfast on the Plains*, painted by the great Western artist Frederick Remington around 1890.

BUFFALO SOLDIERS Troopers of the all-black 10th Cavalry adopt a swaggering pose for this 1894 photograph.

when they were immobilised by winter snows. Summer had been the traditional season for war, since long before the white man came. In the autumn, braves turned from fighting each other to hunting buffalo. In this way, they built up the food hoard which would see them through until spring, when grazing enabled their hunger-weakened ponies to recover. Then the cycle could resume again. The idea of fighting through winter would have seemed inconceivable to Indians and to conventional military men.

The first campaign began in November 1868 under the command of George Armstrong Custer. He not only destroyed an unsuspecting Cheyenne encampment in minutes, but also slaughtered its herd of 700 ponies, denying the few survivors the possibility of fleeing or hunting the following year. The Plains Indians, divided by traditional rivalries, had no answer to such systematic destruction beyond sporadic acts of reprisal.

The US cavalry was, however, far from an efficient war machine. Despite the experience gained by the professional military in the course of the Civil War, the average trooper was often poorly trained and equipped. Not until 1879 were they finally required to practise their marksmanship by firing at least 20 rounds a month. They were routinely issued with unsharpened sabres,

even though garrison armourers often lacked the equipment to give them a proper cutting edge. Most troopers lacked the skill to use them effectively anyway, and on active service sabres were often left behind in barracks as a useless encumbrance. Government meanness and corruption meant that Civil War uniforms and even rations were still being used in the 1880s. Scurvy was common where fruit and vegetables were unobtainable. Sickness of all sorts constantly eroded the strength of frontline garrisons. The annual death rate from wounds or accidents was five in every thousand, with eight in every thousand men succumbing to disease. Venereal diseases and tuberculosis were the most common afflictions, but periodic outbreaks

THE ART OF PERSUASION The cantankerous mule was a mainstay of the army supply system, used to carry goods and equipment over very long distances as the cavalry marched relentlessly onwards.

GOD'S OWN COUNTRY   The dramatic terrain of the West inspired many painters to try to capture its grandeur.

of cholera and dysentery could decimate whole garrisons. Medical services were stretched to their limit. Each medical officer was responsible for up to 250 men, usually assisted by orderlies who had proved themselves useless for anything else.

Due to the rivalry between manufacturers vying for army contracts, troopers were equipped with a bewildering variety of carbines and pistols. The favourite weapons were those which were reliable and stood up to rough treatment, rather than those with the greatest range, accuracy, or rate of fire. The advent of rifles which could be loaded through the breech or from a magazine gave the soldier a decisive advantage over his enemy – by enabling him to reload while lying down or on horseback, greatly increasing his rate of fire. Armed with this

What gave the army a built-in advantage was its ability to rely on stores of grain for their animals, which allowed them to campaign throughout the winter. Their enemies' mounts relied on grass, and so were too poorly nourished for fighting strength. Most army 'victories' came from surprise raids on encampments, when Indian warriors were too distracted by trying to protect their families to be able to fight back effectively. In a war of movement and pursuit, the cavalry were hopelessly outclassed. Such campaigns were, in the words of one saddle-sore trooper, 'like trying to catch the wind'.

OPENING UP THE PLAINS

During the two decades after the ending of the Civil War in 1865, more land was brought into cultivation in the United States than in the previous two-and-a-half centuries, since European settlement had begun along the eastern seaboard. Some of the newcomers were fresh from Europe; of these, the Germans and the Scandinavians were the most experienced farmers. Others were former slaves, driven from the South by persecution or poverty. But the majority were native-born Americans from east of the Mississippi. The most ambitious of these saw that the organisation and development of new territories presented unprecedented opportunities, not only for farmers but also for merchants, bankers and lawyers. The new territories also offered far easier access to political office than in the East, where cash and connections had begun to count more than leather lungs and a way with words. Most of the incomers were would-be farmers. Many were veterans of the Civil War, toughened to hardship, and eager to pit their strength against Native Americans or the elements, in order to make a part of America their own. The railroad companies, which had forged a coast-to-coast link by 1869, did all they could to encourage immigration in their eagerness to generate traffic. By 1883 the Northern Pacific had 124 agents scattered throughout mainland Europe, and no less than 831 in the British Isles. That year its Liverpool office alone poured out half a million copies of its publications in five different languages.

Having taken possession of their land, a pioneer family might initially live as though still travelling, using their wagon or a tent for shelter, but this

sort of weapon, a man could fire at least twice as fast as one with a single-shot muzzle-loader.

Although the cavalry usually had better weapons than the Native Americans, they seldom had better horses and were far less expert at handling them. Apart from their traditional bow, lance, club and tomahawk, the Indians also had firearms, but these were usually old, poorly maintained and liable to backfire. Also, they rarely had enough ammunition for practice, so marksmanship was poor.

ACROSS THE OVERLAND CONTINENT

UNION PACIFIC RAILWAY,
The Pioneer Trans-Continental Route,
TO THE
GREAT CENTRAL SHORT LINE
Between the Missouri River and the Pacific Coast
BETWEEN   BETWEEN
San Francisco   Portland, Ore.

Cheapest, Quickest, Safest and Best Route

NEBRASKA
KANSAS
COLORADO
WYOMING
IDAHO
Utah, Montana, Oregon, Washington Ter.
Nevada and California.

THROUGH EMIGRANT SLEEPING CARS
AND RUN DAILY BETWEEN THE
MISSOURI RIVER and LOS ANGELES, CAL.
REDUCED RATES

ON THE MOVE The laying of railroad tracks across Montana in 1887 was organised on military lines. Left: A Union Pacific poster advertises a daily sleeping-car service for emigrants, linking California to the Missouri.

'soddy' in 1877. It was made in just four days and for a minimal outlay of actual cash: 'I made out an estimate of the cost of our house . . . Ridgepole and hauling (including two loads of firewood) $1.50; rafters and straw 50¢; 2 lb nails 15¢; hinges 20¢; window 75¢; total cash paid – $4.05. Then there was $4 worth of lumber, which was paid for in work, and $1.50 for hauling it over, which, together with hauling the firewood, 50¢, makes $10.05 for a place to live in and firewood to last all summer.' Ruede's satisfaction was short-lived, however, as his house completely collapsed a few weeks later, washed out by a storm. Sod-built houses did have a

would scarcely protect them through the piercing cold of winter. The quickest form of dwelling to fashion was a dugout, carved from a hillside, facing away from the prevailing northerly winds. The open side of the manmade cave could be walled-up with the earth that had been removed to make it, steadied by such timbers as could be spared or scavenged. The resulting refuge was dark and damp, but much more snug than trying to endure a blizzard under canvas.

Freestanding sod houses were usually built in spring, so that the cutting of sod 'bricks' with a hired ox team and a heavy-duty plough would clear the topsoil for cultivation. Howard Ruede, a Pennsylvania-German immigrant to Kansas, described in his letters home how he built his first

THE SPREAD OF THE RAILWAY

Vast areas of land were given to the railway companies by the US government to build rail routes linking East and West. The railway companies then sold much of it in lots to settlers, hoping that as they settled the land and grew crops they would generate freight traffic custom.

major advantage in being virtually fireproof, but they also offered a friendly home to insects, mice, snakes and other vermin. Unless the inner walls were lined with clay and whitewashed with lime, they also tended to shed a constant flow of dust. In 1876 nine-tenths of all the settlers in Butler County, Nebraska, were living in houses made of dirt.

Probably the most comfortable pioneer dwellings were those built in the American southwest, where settlers copied the tried-and-tested adobe houses built by the local people for generations. Bricks made of sun-dried mud and straw, bound together with more mud used as a mortar, were strong enough to withstand even tornadoes.

FRONTIER SOD HOUSE This sod house from 1892 was built into the side of a bluff. Such houses were damp in winter, dusty in summer and dark all year round. The wagon-load of cut sods is for repairing the roof.

Dr Cass G. Barns moved from Indiana to Nebraska in 1878. As a doctor he was acutely aware of the invisible dangers which were inseparable from the unhygienic necessities of the first stage of pioneering: 'It was not wholly the fault of the sod house that contagious diseases were common. The common drinking cup, the open dug well, the outdoor toilet – or no toilet at all – shared the blame with the lack of ventilation and crowded quarters of the sod house.' As Dr Barns was himself fully aware from personal experience, a dirt floor could not be scrubbed clean or disinfected. Spitting was not understood to constitute a health hazard. Fleas and bed bugs were noticeable only when they were absent. He concluded that: 'Added to the lowering of vitality by lack of a balanced ration of food, lack of clothing, and changes of temperature, the wonder is not so much that disease and infection took a heavy toll, as the wonder that

A FRONTIER HOUSEWIFE: BACK TO BASICS

AS IT IS HIGH SUMMER, Molly Gray is thankful to be able to clear the menfolk out as soon as breakfast is done. Two of the boys go off with a gun and a wheelbarrow, hoping to bag a rabbit or a quail and under orders to fill the barrow with 'chips' of dried buffalo dung used to fuel the pot-bellied iron stove. In the depths of winter, when the snow lies too deep for gathering chips, they will burn corncobs and chopped-up sunflower stalks. The stove is Molly's pride and joy and a lifesaver in this open country, where wood is too scarce and expensive to burn freely on a wasteful hearth. Sarah, her oldest daughter, is set to making her first batch of soap. She has patiently trickled water through an old barrel of wood ash to leach out the potash; today she will boil this in a kettle with salt, bacon rinds and scraps of fat saved from the kitchen waste, then mould the residue into little cakes. This will be an economical way of using surplus heat from the

KITCHENWARE **The frontier housewife's essential kitchen utensils, such as this heavy iron stewpot and stoneware jug, were simple and sturdy.**

FUEL GATHERING **Before the great buffalo herds were wiped out, the pioneers used the dried buffalo dung for fuel. Women would go out to gather up the buffalo 'chips'.**

stove, which Molly is stoking up so that she can make biscuits – a daily task. David, the youngest boy, is deputed to drag a half-empty sack of flour from an outhouse. Meanwhile, Molly rinses her hands in a tin bowl. While she mixes the biscuit dough, David is set to keeping the stove stoked up. It is an unpleasantly smoky, sweaty chore for a little boy on a warm day. Molly cuts out biscuits with the top of an old baking-powder can and then consigns them to the oven compartment of the stove.

Molly glances down at her son's shirt. Although clean on that morning, it still looks grubby and she resolves to have Sarah wash it, once her soap is hardened, so that he can look decent at Sunday service. Without some sort of soap, washing pounded at the creek still ends up looking what her neighbour calls 'clean for brown but awful dirty for white'.

After the baking is done, the stove is still warm. Molly uses the heat to melt tallow, which is then poured into a mould carved from a block of wood, into which wicks, made from unpicked sacking, are laid. These candles smell as they glimmer feebly, but on a winter's evening they give enough light for Molly to mend by.

In the afternoon a rare but welcome visitor comes. 'Irish Joe' is a travelling tinker and a godsend to housewives, for whom a cracked pan is a domestic disaster. He works a wide but regular circuit, and is as valued for the gossip he passes from one end of the county to the other as he is for his skills. Molly wisely makes a fuss of him and offers him real coffee, unadulterated by parched corn to 'stretch it'. Joe is also something of a pedlar but sticks to lightweight necessities, such as needles, fish-hooks and strong twine.

As evening draws on, Molly organises the main meal of the day, when all her family will assemble. Afterwards, for as long as the light lasts, she takes the younger children through some of Webster's 'speller' and the older ones through a selection from McGuffey's *Eclectic Reader*. As darkness falls, she contemplates with weary satisfaction the sole luxury of her life, the present that her family smuggled from the railway – a proper bed, with a real mattress.

so many survived to spend their later lives in modern homes.' These health reasons, together with drought or the destruction of crops by pests, were the main reasons why so many settlers failed.

A New Kind of Farming

The pioneers had a hard time of it learning how to farm the prairie successfully. The earliest settlers were hampered by their ignorance of its climate and soil, the type of crops it would support and the best ways of growing them. Out on the central plains, rainfall averaged only 15 in (38 cm) a year; most fell between April and November, when it was evaporated by the hot summer sun and warm winds. Digging a shaft 480 ft (146 m) deep might locate underground water, but this was insufficient to irrigate a typical 160 acre (65 ha) farm. Large as this was by European standards, such an acreage was still not big enough to support a family when yields were so much lower than in the East, where moisture was far more abundant. There were other hazards, too, such as summer hailstorms and brush fires.

In the 1870s there was a plague of grasshoppers. More than 60 years later an 'old-timer' recalled the devastation he had witnessed in his youth: 'The cornstalks . . . were as naked as beanpoles . . . Fruit hung on the leafless branches, gnawed to the core. The woods looked thin as in late autumn. Water troughs and loosely covered wells were fouled with drowned "hoppers". A young wife, awaiting her first baby in the absence of her husband, had gone insane from fright. . . .'

The disastrous experiences of the decade after the Civil War caused a radical rethink in farming methods on the plains. Technology came to the rescue with improved and much cheaper mechanical reapers, binders and threshers. With a self-binding harvester one man could do the work of six. Barbed wire solved the problem of fencing. Wind pumps utilised the constant prairie breezes to raise water from deep underground. The evolution of 'dry farming' techniques, such as turning the land after a shower or snowfall to seal in the moisture, helped to make the most efficient use of precipitation. Doubling the size of holdings to 320 acres (129 ha) enabled farmers to let acreage lie fallow, rather than pulverising it to dust by repeated cropping. In 1874 immigrants from the Crimea brought 'Turkey Red', a hard winter wheat which could resist frost and proved ideal on the plains.

But, with much determination and a little luck, a family could progress from primitive conditions to relative comfort in less than a generation. Willa Cather (1873-1947) spent her childhood in Nebraska,

MECHANISATION The huge imbalance between land and the manpower available to cultivate it encouraged the invention of machinery, such as this lightweight horse-drawn hoe (above). Right: Steam power made possible the development of large-scale mechanised operations.

FLIGHT OF FANCY Cartoonists ridiculed the mad rush to California for what often turned out to be fool's gold.

which provided the setting for her novel *O Pioneers!* Alexandra Bergson, its Swedish heroine, battles against debt and drought to hold onto the family homestead after the early death of her father. After more than a decade of exhausting toil, the Bergsons had still scarcely scratched the surface of the soil and lived in a single-storey log cabin. However, 15 years later, in the late 1890s, the Bergsons were farming an area five times larger than their original holding, with each acre worth ten times what they had originally paid for it – and Alexandra was living in a gracious house, cluttered with fashionable ornaments.

THE MINERS AND THE GOLD RUSH

By the time Alcalde (Mayor) John Colton recorded the impact of 'gold fever' on his town of Monterey in June 1848, California had been in its grip for six months: 'I have only a community of women left, and a gang of prisoners, with here and there a soldier, who will give his captain the slip at the first chance.' A month later, Colton noted with disgust, but little surprise, that he and the local military commandant had been reduced to cooking their own breakfast because all their official and personal staff had deserted them: 'These gold mines are going to upset all the domestic arrangements of society, turning the head to the tail, and the tail to the head.' Three days later, the arrival in town of an ex-sailor with a fist-sized bag of gold dust touched off 'another spasm' among what was left of

NO GOLDEN DREAM Racism drove many Chinese from the actual diggings to seek economic survival as cooks or laundrymen. Later, many found employment in railroad construction.

THE FAR WEST AND THE PLAINS

DID YOU KNOW?

It has been estimated that by 1868 the primitive mining and panhandling methods used by the early prospectors had lost beyond recovery nearly $300 million worth of precious metals.

George Pullman, the future builder of Pullman railway cars, is said to have got the idea for his luxury 'sleeper' trains when he was a prospector in Colorado in 1859 and saw miners sleeping in double-decked bunks.

the *Washington Daily Union* published a letter from a correspondent in Monterey, describing the raging inflation which was another effect of the communal madness: 'You can hardly hire a labourer here for $10 a day, and on the gold river he charges $50 . . . Tin pans have found a ready sale at $8 each; shovels at $10; a trough scooped out of a log, with a willow sieve in it, $100 . . . The price of

the local population. A whole gang of carpenters abandoned the half-built schoolhouse. Three seamen deserted a man-of-war, forfeiting four years of back-pay, and a platoon abandoned their fort, leaving the flag to fly over a garrison of ghosts.

News of the gold rush only became generally known in the East in August 1848. In September

THE SEARCH FOR GOLD
Above: A solitary prospector patiently pans for gold by hand. Left: A team works a sluice box. This diverted a water source and allowed them to wash out the mined 'dirt' with a constant stream of water. Such simple levels of 'mechanisation' greatly improved productivity, compared with the more hit-and-miss method of panning.

REVELRY The absence of women at this 'miners' ball' at Cripple Creek, Colorado, in 1891 failed to inhibit enthusiastic dancing to the sound of a 'squeezebox' and the hoarse instructions of a caller.

board on the gold streams is $3 a day. For this the boarder gets coarse bread, beef and beans, a tree to sleep under, and an owl to hoot in his ear at night. The gold is sold here for $14 the ounce (28 g) and is worth $18 at any mint.'

The simple technology of processing the 'pay dirt' – from where the phrase originates – progressed rapidly. The most basic method of recovering gold was to swirl the dirt around in a pan of water until the heavier specks of gold dust were separated from the mud and gravel and could be scraped from the bottom of the pan. The 'cradle', an improved version of the plain washing pan, had cleats to catch the gold, so that it could be rocked with one hand while a stream of dirt and water was fed in with the other. Better still was the 'sluice box', a

EYEWITNESS

CULTURE AND ANARCHY: AN AESTHETE AT RISK

IN 1882 Oscar Wilde toured America and Canada, exhorting audiences to cherish art. He met with ridicule and bemusement, but not even the miners of Leadville, Colorado, could upset his sardonic equanimity:

❦ I was told that if I went there they would be sure to shoot me or my travelling manager. I wrote and told them that nothing they could do to my travelling manager would intimidate me. They are miners – men working in metals, so I lectured them on the Ethics of Art. I read them passages from the *Autobiography of Benvenuto Cellini*, and they seemed most delighted. I was reproved by my hearers for not having brought him with me. I explained that he had been dead for

JUST DANDY Oscar Wilde's flamboyant posturings outraged London society, but they were met with amused tolerance by miners – who welcomed any distraction.

some little time, which elicited the enquiry "Who shot him?" They afterwards took me to a dancing saloon where I saw the only rational method of art criticism I have ever come across. Over the piano was printed a notice:

PLEASE DO NOT SHOOT THE PIANIST HE IS DOING HIS BEST

The mortality among pianists in that place is marvellous. Then they asked me to supper, and having accepted, I had to descend a mine in a rickety bucket in which it was impossible to be graceful. Having got into the heart of the mountain I had supper, the first course being whisky, the second whisky and the third whisky. ❦

coffin-like contraption with cleats at one of its two open ends, which was placed so that a stream could be diverted through it to provide a constant flow of washing water. The miner then shovelled dirt into the top, let the stream pulsate through it, and periodically collected the gold that was trapped.

The California gold rush gave birth to a way of life which lasted for half a century as prospectors moved north, south and east to find fortunes. The discovery of gold near Denver, Colorado, in 1858 prompted a swift about-turn as 100 000 'fiftyniners' headed south. Then came Nevada, followed by Montana, Idaho, Arizona, New Mexico and South Dakota. Each created communities whose crudeness and violence horrified visitors.

Newspaperman Horace Greeley recorded of Denver in 1859 that: 'I apprehend that there have been, during my two weeks sojourn, more brawls, more fights, more pistol shots with criminal intent in this log city of one hundred and fifty dwellings, not three-fourths completed, nor two-thirds inhabited, nor one-third fit to be, than in any community of no greater numbers on earth.'

A typical claim, which had to be registered, ran from one side of a gulch to the other and was 100 ft (30 m) wide. But the efficient exploitation required deep-mining and ore-crushing technologies, which involved capital investments far beyond the resources or imagination of the amateur fortune-seeker. In the long run it was the corporations that made the biggest killings.

TOUGH GUY Nat Love, nicknamed 'Deadwood Nick', is the subject of this photograph from the 1880s. Almost a third of all cowboys were black or Mexican.

The last major strike was at Rabbit (later Bonanza) Creek, in 1896, which touched off the Klondike Rush in the autumn of 1897, attracting 100 000 gold-seekers. For those who had to travel overland, it took two years to get to the Klondike River, which flowed through the Yukon Territory in Canada. By the time they arrived, Dawson, at the mouth of the Klondike River, had become the largest community west of Winnipeg and boasted such modern sophistications as electricity, telephones and even movie houses. In the summer of 1899 rumours of yet another gold find, at Nome in Alaska, redirected the stampede even farther north.

Mining encouraged the settlement of areas too remote or infertile for the farmer and boosted the development of transport and commerce as men – and women – of enterprise rushed to cash in on the miners' demands for food, equipment and recreation. Not least of all, the succession of strikes and rushes sustained a bonanza mentality – a belief that, in the land of endless opportunity, a fortune was always just around the corner for anyone with the energy, the

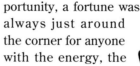

COWBOY KIT A genuine broad-brimmed Stetson cost more than a month's wages but could also be used as a bucket or a pillow. A cowboy's saddle was so essential to his livelihood that it was the last thing he would sell, pawn or gamble.

HORSE TRAINING   Breaking in the wild mustangs, as on this horse ranch in the Midwest, was dangerous work.

tenacity or indeed, the imagination to wrest it from nature.

Like the miner, the cattleman hoped to make his fortune from nature's bounty – and had a far better chance of doing so. Cows harvested a free crop of grass, processed it into beef and hides, transported those commodities to market on the hoof and very often dropped calves along the way to replace themselves. Even the cattle's horns and bones could be ground down and sold as fertiliser.

CATTLEMEN AND COWBOYS
In the brief interval between the destruction of the Native Americans and the consolidation of settled agriculture, the Great Plains provided the stage for the world's most picturesque industrial drama – the rise and fall of the cattle bonanza. The range represented wealth for the taking and the bison which had once sustained an entire culture were slaughtered to make way for herds of cattle.

As the miner moved into the mountains from the West, so the rancher invaded from the South, bringing a Mexican-flavoured horse-bound lifestyle which had evolved in Texas. The cowboy saddle, rowelled spurs, high-heeled boots, broad-brimmed hat, lasso and protective 'chaps' were all Mexican (and initially Spanish) in origin.

On the eve of the Civil War in 1860, the census estimated that there were 3.5 million cattle in Texas; by the end there were 5 million. A cow which could be bought for $3-$5 in Texas could be sold for ten times as much in the North. For safety against armed raiders, drovers generally kept to the open plains. Conditions were hard on the men – few herds were as yet accompanied by chuck wagons, and hands had to live on what they could carry and cook themselves. Many lived entirely on beef for the last weeks of the drive when their supplies ran out. There were no tents to shelter them and few had long 'slickers', proofed with linseed oil, to keep off the rain. Most cowboys owned nothing but their horse, saddle, gun and clothes; some had to borrow them and work off the debt in the course of the drive. A saddle was the cowhand's most valuable possession – at $40-$50 it represented two months' wages. Cowboys were wiry and

GIT ALOOONG!   On the trail from Texas to Abilene, the drover's life was one of long hours of boredom and sudden moments of danger.

endowed with great stamina: their average age was 24.

In 1867 Abilene in Kansas was founded specifically to receive cows for shipment onwards to the slaughterhouses of Chicago. Its founder, Joseph G. McCoy, remembers that its first year's success was hard won: 'Great hardships attended driving that year on account of Osage Indian troubles, excessive rainstorms and flooded rivers. The cholera made sad havoc with many drovers . . . The heavy rains caused an immense growth of grass, too coarse and washy to be good food . . . and but little of the first year's arrivals at Abilene were fit to go to market.' Later cow towns – Wichita, Ellsworth, Dodge City, Cheyenne and Laramie – pushed farther westward with the railroad. Like the 'cities' which sprang up around the mining camps, these were violent places and acted as magnets for the gambler, thief and whore. Twenty-five men were killed in Dodge City in its first year of existence.

Of the 6 million head of cattle driven north between 1866 and 1888, by no means all went directly to market. Some were used to stock the south-west and the Great Plains. Others went to feed the mining camps, railroad crews, Indian reservations and the wagon trains of emigrants. Cattle-raising on the open range was wasteful and inefficient. Unfenced animals were exposed to the hazards of disease, severe weather and rustlers, and bloody disputes over rights of grazing and passage were inevitable. The cattle barons sometimes resorted to land fraud, corruption and ruthless intimidation. Worse still, they overstocked, overgrazed and over-produced. Beef prices began to tumble in 1885. Then

BRAND NEW The Becker sisters brand cattle in 1894. After the death of their father, the sisters carried on running the family ranch in the San Luis Valley, Colorado.

nature intervened with a winter so savage that some herds on the southern ranges lost up to 85 per cent of their number, frozen or starved to death. A scorching drought followed. Then another winter, even worse. The cattlemen learned the hard way that it was better to play safe.

As one cowboy wistfully recalled: 'I remember when we sat around the fire the winter through and didn't do a lick of work for five or six months . . . Now we go on the general roundup, then the calf roundup, then comes haying – something that the old time cowboy never dreamed of – then the beef roundup, and the Fall calf roundup and gathering bulls and weak cows, and after all this a winter feeding of hay. I tell you times have changed.'

WIPED OUT Drought was the rancher's worst nightmare and they were helpless if the rains failed to arrive. Many cattle had to be left to die in times of drought – making rich pickings for the vultures.

THE RABBIT-HOLE SPRINGS,

THE MAKING OF A CIVILISATION

The first pioneers moved to leave the settled life of the East behind them.

Their successors ultimately sought to re-create it. The clapboard church and the one-room

schoolhouse were as much the weapons of settlement as the rifle and plough.

THE REVEREND Timothy Flint liked the frontiersmen of the Mississippi valley, despite the fact that their estimation of his calling was pretty low: 'They care little about ministers and think less about paying them.' A mild-mannered New Englander, he had gone to the frontier with the greatest apprehension, having heard 'a thousand stories of gougings, and robberies and shooting down with the rifle'. But, when he published his *Recollections of the Last Ten Years* in 1826, he was able to inform his Bostonian readers that, in all his miles of wanderings, he had never carried a weapon and never felt in need of protection. Although he met with generous hospitality everywhere he went, early frontier life was essentially hostile to Flint's cultivated brand of religion. Settlers were poor, scattered, isolated and battling

MAIN STREET Cattle amble through Barkerville in British Columbia. The town boasted both a church and an imposing balconied house. Such towns, built entirely from wood, were very vulnerable to fire.

FRONTIER FERVOUR   At a well-ordered outdoor Methodist gathering, the men and women sit separately.

daily for sheer survival. Their habit of moving on every few seasons weakened any interest they might have had in creating or supporting permanent institutions, including religious ones. Religious groups which equated spiritual progress with fine buildings serviced by paid clergy were doomed to disappointment. But the pioneers did respond to those which brought colour and excitement into their world of drudgery and loneliness.

'Revivalism', with its high emotional charge, had swept through the back country of the American colonies as early as the 1730s, and was to do so repeatedly along the moving frontier. Its most distinctive feature was the 'camp meeting'. Settlers would walk as many as 30 miles (48 km) to form a large, if temporary, congregation, which would stay together for days at a time. Most camp meetings were organised after the harvest and before the winter set in. The concourse at Cane Ridge, Kentucky, in August 1801 drew an estimated 25 000 people. James Finley, later one of the most famous of all backwoods preachers, was converted at this gathering. Singing, praying or just shouting, an exhilarated mob of thousands could raise a noise 'like the roar of Niagara', as Finley put it. Being caught up in such a throng was a tremendous experience for most of its members, for it would have been by far the largest crowd they had ever been part of and far larger than the population of any frontier town. Excitement provoked emotional excesses, like 'the jerks', recorded near Knoxville, Tennessee in 1803:

'Hundreds of men and women would commence jerking backward and forward with great rapidity and violence so that their bodies would bend so as to bring their heads near to the floor, and the hair of the women would crack like the lash of a driver's whip.' Some barked like dogs, while others gave way to uncontrollable laughter or weeping, manic rolling, shaking or dancing or states of ecstatic trance.

METHODIST MOMENTUM

Some sects prospered far better than others, their success depending on the tone of their teaching. Frontier optimism and informality chimed with the hopeful gregariousness of the Methodists and Baptists, who stressed the importance of a dramatic conversion and salvation through free will, rather than the gloomy Calvinism

RIDE ON, RIDE ON . . . A Methodist circuit-rider battles through the mountains of Kentucky to spread the Word of God. Despite atrocious conditions, he keeps to his formal clerical dress.

of New England, or the stress on hierarchy and ritual associated with the Roman Catholics or the Anglicans. Methodist ministers on the frontier were 'circuit riders', serving populations scattered over immense areas and preaching as their founder John Wesley had done in courthouses, schools and private homes, or even under a tree in the open air. The number of formally committed Methodists in the USA rose from 8504 in 1780 to 174 560 by 1810; but a far larger number took part in their services because many pioneers were willing to listen to any preacher who came along. Frontiersmen respected the ministers' emphasis on being teetotal, but largely ignored their advice. By 1870 the Methodists were the largest of all American denominations, with 25 278 congregations – far ahead of the Baptists (15 829), Presbyterians (7824) and Catholics (4127).

THEORY AND PRACTICE

Despite the separation of Church and state proclaimed by the American constitution, it was widely assumed that religion and good order went hand-in-hand. Repeated attempts were made to legislate morality and enforce the Puritan Sunday – and proved repeatedly futile. In 1804 the Ohio assembly tried to ban quarrelling, shooting and working on Sundays, prohibited gambling and proposed to fine blasphemers. In Uvalde, Texas, a prudent

FROM ABOLITION TO PROHIBITION The campaign against slavery attracted many women into the public arena for the first time. Fired with success, many went on to crusade against another evil – alcohol.

Parson Potter made it his practice to lay his pistol down alongside his Bible in the pulpit and warn his congregation that 'the first fellow that makes a move while I am preaching I'm going to shoot him right between the eyes – and I'm a good shot'. As well as the cults which originated in Europe and

PASSION AND PRECISION The fervour of Shaker prayer meetings alarmed outsiders. Above: The quality of Shaker design and craftsmanship, as typified by this chair, was widely admired.

found a new home in the New World, there were dozens of Utopian communities of purely American origin, many of which were also organised along socialist or communist lines. For the most part, their founders hoped to establish a working model of social perfection to serve as the example and catalyst for a wholesale reformation of American society.

Fearful of the outside world, these various religious communities distanced themselves from it by denying liability to military service, avoiding litigation, growing their own food, and making their own clothing and other basic commodities such as paper, candles and soap. Some sects endured for decades but most disintegrated after a few years, usually following the death of the leader who held them together, or through some doctrinal squabble.

SHAKERS AND SOCIALISTS

The largest and most permanent of the religious commune movements was officially called the United Society of Believers, but usually referred to as the Shakers, because they danced to shake sin from their bodies through their fingertips. Initially led by an illiterate English prophetess, Ann Lee Stanley, who emigrated to America in 1774, the Shakers eventu-

ally had about 6000 members in 20 settlements in seven states. 'Mother Ann's' own loveless experience of marriage led her to the conclusion that a consummated union was 'a covenant with death and an agreement with hell'. All Shakers had to adhere to a strict code of celibacy as 'filthy gratification' was forbidden. Men worked in the fields, women in the house. They slept in separate dormitories and ate at separate tables. Even conversation was formally supervised, with lines of 'brothers' and 'sisters' sitting opposite each other in rows. Shaker houses were renowned for their neatness and order, and Shaker furniture was celebrated for its strength, simplicity and elegance. In time, the Shakers turned their industrious hands to producing goods for the outside world. The high standards of Shaker craftsmanship and productivity were an impressive demonstration of the value of corporate effort in a century which tended to praise only individual effort and admired buccaneering

PROPHET IN THE WILDERNESS
The former carpenter and joiner from Vermont, Brigham Young (left), led the Mormons outside the boundaries of the United States to found Salt Lake City, shown below in 1853.

MORMON LIVES: HARD GRAFT ON THE WAY TO HEAVEN

HORACE GREELEY, editor of the New York Tribune, paid a visit to the Mormon kingdom 12 years after its beginnings and thought the saints were having a tough time of it:

❛ These Mormons are in the main an industrious, frugal, hard-working people. Few of them are habitual idlers; few live by professions or pursuits that require no physical exertion. They make work for but few lawyers . . . Utah has not a single export of any kind . . . up to this hour, her manufacturing energies have been most unhappily directed. Some $200 000 was expended in preparations for iron making . . . but the ore, though rich, would not flux, and the enterprise had to be totally abandoned . . . An attempt to grow cotton is likely to prove a failure . . . Sugar is another necessary of life which they have had bad luck with. They can grow the beet very well, but it is said to yield little or no sugar – because, it is supposed, of an excess of alkali in the soil . . . The houses are uniformly low and generally too small; but there is seldom more than one family to a dwelling . . . The gardens are well filled with peach, apple and other fruit trees . . . Undoubtedly this people are steadily increasing in wealth and comfort. Still the average life in Utah is a hard one . . . The climate is severe and capricious . . . Wood is scarce and poor. Irrigation is laborious and expensive; as yet, it has not been found practicable to irrigate one-fourth of the arable land . . . 150 days' faithful labour in Kansas will produce as large an aggregate of the necessaries of life – food, clothing, fuel – as 300 just such days' work in Utah . . . The adults here generally wear a toil-worn, anxious look, and many of them are older in frame than in years. ❜

FAMILY LIFE   The Mormons' commitment to polygamy scandalised other Americans and precluded Utah from entering the Union until it had been renounced.

business methods. However, due to the strict rules of celibacy, by 1905 their numbers were down to about 1000, and by the 1970s there was only a handful of elderly female survivors.

THE MORMONS

America's most successful Utopian experiment was entirely home-grown. The Church of Jesus Christ of Latter-Day Saints was founded by an American prophet, Joseph Smith, and built around a revelation made in America to Americans – *The Book of Mormon* – which only Smith could read. Smith 'translated' the original and then claimed to have returned the text to the angel who had brought it to him. Displaying the quintessential frontier virtues of energy and enterprise, Mormons practised polygamy, which meant that the men were able to take two or more wives – although the women could not have more than one husband.

Smith's followers endured a decade and a half of bloody persecution, which chased them from Ohio to Missouri to Illinois, before their leader's murder at the hands of a mob – for preaching polygamy – launched them into the wilderness.

In February 1846, Smith's successor, Brigham Young, set the entire community on a trek to the West, to an unknown destination and destiny. The direction of their well-disciplined march was intended to take them outside the boundaries of the United States. In August 1847 they halted on an arid, treeless plateau surrounded by hills. Young announced: 'This is the place.' Salt Lake City was founded there, and soon colonies were being established throughout the surrounding area which ironically, as a result of the Mexican War of 1846-8, became US territory soon afterwards. Not until the Mormons had renounced polygamy in 1896 was their 'Kingdom of Deseret' (Land of the Honey

GOD'S CHILDREN Although many miners favoured violent distractions, gambling and drunkenness, some were God-fearing men who welcomed the visits of a wandering preacher.

Bee) admitted into the Union as the State of Utah.

Meanwhile, the Mormons worked ferociously to build a heaven on earth. A young English convert, Frederick Piercy from Liverpool, recorded how in their first year at a new settlement called 'Parowan City', the pioneers constructed an 8 mile (13 km) road; bridged a creek at six different points; built homes, a two-storey meeting house, a fort, a sawmill and a gristmill; dug 30 miles (48 km) of canals and ditches; and fenced off a vast field 3 miles (5 km) long and 5 miles (8 km) broad. By using the water from mountain streams to irrigate the land, the Mormons eventually established flourishing farms, and in 30 years their numbers rose, by immigration and natural increase, from 6000 to 200 000. They had found – or rather, made – their Promised Land.

THE CODE OF THE WEST

The Mormons may have fled to escape persecution, but that did not prevent them from perpetrating the largest slaughter of white civilians in the history of the West. Threatened by the approach of a US army expeditionary force in 1857, the Mormons, reinforced by a band of Paiute Indians, fell upon a California-bound wagon train of Arkansans, killing some 100 people in what became known as the Mountain Meadows Massacre. Only 18 of the younger children were spared.

Inter-ethnic violence could be quite as deadly. In 1872 a feud among the Cherokee of what is now

RACE RIOT This anti-Chinese riot in Denver, Colorado, in 1880 was symptomatic of the current xenophobia, although miners generally accepted migrants from Europe.

eastern Oklahoma became entangled with a dispute about the respective jurisprudence of Indian and federal courts. An attempted resolution by armed force led to a shoot-out costing 11 lives, eight of them US deputies. The Chinese were a particular target for mob hatred, especially in mining camps. Not surprisingly, most Chinese gave up mining in favour of railroad construction, laundry work and catering.

If nonwhites could seldom expect the protection of the law, whites were often content to make their own. Wagon trains, for example, evolved their own system of instant justice. Juries were usually selected by lot, with the accused, witnesses and their messmates excluded. Minor offences required a jury of only five, the verdict depending on a simple majority and the penalty being decided by the same jury. Petty infringements such as gambling might be punished by extra spells of guard duty.

THE SWIFT RETRIBUTION OF FRONTIER JUSTICE

BY 1866 there were over 1100 officially recognised 'Mining Districts' in the mineral-rich West. Their mushroom growth posed entirely new problems of law and order, and forced men to invent their own solutions. Remote from legally constituted authority, the miners established 'Vigilance Committees' and 'People's Courts' – not to bypass existing institutions but to remedy their absence.

Most miners had a deep suspicion of lawyers, but considered the need for law to be self-evident. Men went to the diggings to get rich, but they could only do this if their right to what they discovered was respected.

Each camp laid down its own simple rules to define the size of legitimate claims and how they could be registered, transferred or forfeited. Theft and violence met swift retribution. The absence of paid officials and paid lawyers meant that long or complex proceedings were in no one's interest. As there were no prisons, the standard punishments were whipping, banishment or hanging.

Since 'courts' were far less punctilious about keeping records of proceedings and verdicts than they were about registering claims and transfers, a special debt of gratitude is owed to 'Professor' Thomas J. Dimsdale, an Oxford-educated Englishman who drew on his first-hand experience of a 'People's Court' in Virginia City to produce the Idaho Territory's first published work, *Vigilantes of Montana*. Published in 1866, Dimsdale's account records one particular case which exemplified the swiftness of popular retribution. Murder, arraignment, trial and execution all took place within the space of 58 minutes.

PUNISHMENT There were three main forms of legal punishment – whipping, banishment and hanging.

Threatening the life of another resulted in expulsion, with only enough supplies to reach the nearest settlement. A condemned person often retained the right to appeal to the company as a whole; a positive vote of two-thirds was sufficient to set aside the verdict of a jury, except in the case of murder. For murder, 12 jurors and a unanimous verdict were deemed essential. If three successive juries failed to agree, the accused was acquitted. In case of conviction, the penalty was death – carried out immediately.

Although some states had highly effective mobile crime-fighting forces such as the legendary Texas Rangers and their counterparts in Arizona, many organisations, such as Wells Fargo and the Southern Pacific Railroad, set up and recruited their own private police forces. 'Cattle barons' hired 'regulators' to drive homesteaders from their land, and

HIGHWAY ROBBERY During the 1870s 'road agent' Bill Brazelton robbed stagecoaches in the Arizona Territory – until a posse abruptly terminated his career.

business leaders brought in the Pinkerton Agency plainclothes men to harass attempts at unionisation in mines, mills and logging camps. In 1880 at Mussel Slough, California, an attempt to evict homesteaders led to one of the deadliest civilian gunfights in Western history. Five pioneers were shot dead, but so also were both of the gunfighters hired by the Southern Pacific. News of the incident was reported as far away as London, where Karl Marx vilified it as naked class oppression; it also inspired no less than five novels and led to considerable public sympathy for bandits who subsequently preyed on railroad traffic.

Because the frontier had been 'settled' by violent

LAWMEN   In the absence of adequate policing, wealthy ranchers, powerful railroad corporations and companies such as Wells Fargo organised their own private police forces (right), recruiting ex-soldiers, ex-lawmen and sometimes ex-criminals. Above: Some tools of the trade.

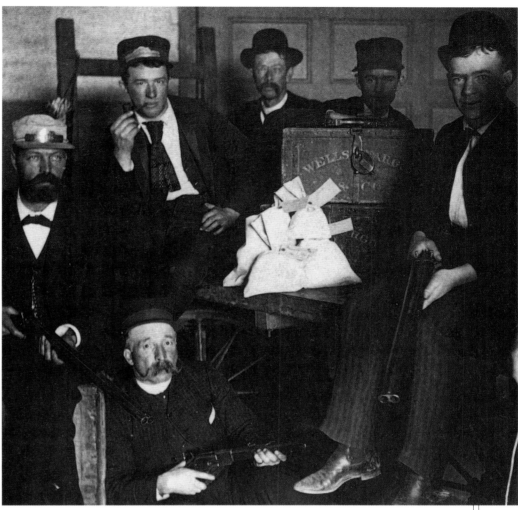

conquest, violence continued to characterise its distinctive society. Both public opinion and the courts upheld the right, indeed the duty, of a man to defend his land, family and personal honour with a gun. Even lynching could meet with semiofficial approval. In 1879 a Denver newspaper stated that a hanging by a vigilante mob in nearby Golden had been not only 'well merited but a positive gain to the county, saving it at least five or six thousand dollars'.

Recourse to properly constituted courts on the frontier was hampered by the huge distances and foul weather. Migratory judges rode 'circuits', just like Methodist preachers. But if they arrived too long after the crimes they were liable to find either that essential witnesses had all moved on or that the community had taken matters into its own hands. In one 15 month period in Los Angeles County (population 8000) in the 1850s, there were 44 homicides, but only one person was brought to trial and he was found 'not guilty'. Nor was the presence of a qualified judge a necessary guarantee that the legal niceties would be observed. One Iowa justice of the peace battered a prisoner so badly that he felt obliged to report, and try, himself. He also acquitted himself.

Underlying the seeming randomness of everyday violence there was a very definite pattern of change. The Earps and Hickoks who 'cleaned up' riotous 'cow towns' like Abilene and Dodge City

'BE JUST AND FEAR NOT'   This elaborate certificate of authority to enforce the law was issued 'In the Name of the People' by the San Francisco Vigilance Committee.

CITY OF THE FUTURE **In 1885, Mullinville, Kansas, was just three months old and in the early stages of being built.**

did so not only so that respectable ladies might walk the streets unmolested, but so that business might prosper in a predictable manner.

FROM SETTLEMENT TO CITY

Prosperous businesses stimulated urban growth. By 1890 the proportion of residents of America's western states who lived in towns of 10 000 or more was larger than that of any other region except the north-east. In *The Winning of the West,* published in 1896, the future president Theodore Roosevelt noted that when Kentucky had become a state in the 1790s, only 1 per cent of its people lived in Lexington, its largest city; when Colorado achieved statehood in the 1870s, no less than a third of its population lived in Denver.

Although Western city planners followed Eastern traditions in their devotion to the regular grid plan and right-angled street layout, they had a larger canvas to work on. New York's streets averaged 60 ft (18 m) across. In the West, 80 ft (24 m) was the norm. In Omaha, 100 ft (30 m) was the standard width, and in Salt Lake City 132 ft (40 m)

STEAM-POWERED **19th-century steam power promised progress and prosperity. The steamboats in this 1850s' picture of St Louis show how the city prospered from trade provided by the Mississippi.**

SIR SANDFORD FLEMING

Sir Sandford Fleming, the chief engineer of the Canadian Pacific Railway, was also responsible for convening the 1884 Washington Conference, which standardised international time zones based on Greenwich time in England. Fleming also urged the building of a Pacific telegraph cable to link Canada and Australia. This engineering feat was completed in 1902. In addition to these endeavours, Sir Sandford Fleming also found the time to design Canada's first postage stamp – the 3 cent 'beaver'.

– plus 20 ft (6 m) sidewalks on each side. Such boulevards provided enough space for teams of wagons not only to pass comfortably, but also to turn right around – though their inspiration was the expression of a common taste for the monumental. As the English journalist G.A. Sala observed with weary incredulity: 'Every town in the West is laid out on a plan so vast as though it were destined, at no distant date, to contain a million of inhabitants.'

Urban growth was, however, seldom a question of smooth and steady progress. Calgary became Alberta's first incorporated town in 1884, the year after the Canadian Pacific Railway established a stop there. By 1893 it had achieved city status. In the first decade of the new century, Calgary's population grew by 1000 per cent. In 1900 Regina had a population of just 2250. In 1905 it was designated capital of the new province of Saskatchewan, and by 1911 it had a population of 30 000.

Denver, which came to call itself the 'Queen City of the Plains and the Rockies', began as a gold rush camp in 1859. Once a railroad link had been established in 1870, the city really began to grow: the population increased seven-fold in the 1870s and trebled again in the following decade to pass the 100 000 mark. By 1881 an easterner could declare that 'there are shops that would do credit to Broadway'. Oscar Wilde observed sardonically in 1882 that the inhabitants of Denver were: 'Ready but not rough . . . The revolver is their book of etiquette. This teaches lessons that are not forgotten.' Denver's civic amenities now included parks, a college, a seminary and an opera house. A British visitor in

COUNTER CHAOS A cartoon of 1886 captures the feel of a station lunchroom. Hasty stops were essential before the advent of dining cars, but train staff sometimes cut them short so that uneaten food could be re-sold to passengers on the next train.

POWER HOUSE   A small town's newspaper office generally housed its only printing press, which gave the editors a lucrative sideline for the printing of official notices, handbills and advertisements.

1885 was impressed by the self-assurance that underlay the scattered location of major public projects: 'Instead of its new streets and buildings being huddled together as with us in our urban beginnings, they are placed here and there at suitable points, with a confidence that the connecting links will soon be established.' They were. By the late 1880s, Denver had cable cars running along 38 miles (61 km) of its streets. By 1890 it was the third largest city in the West.

CIVILISING INFLUENCES

As the frontier of agrarian settlement was officially declared closed, a new frontier, urban and urbane, opened to offer the next generation of migrants another land of opportunity.

As each newly formed community grew and bedded itself in, its need for a social infrastructure grew, too. Churches, schools and meeting houses were built and, as time went on, hotels were opened, colleges were founded and regional newspapers were published. The Scottish traveller James Stirling observed in the 1860s how, on the thinly populated frontier, the Press assumed the role performed by gossip in more settled and stable societies. Moving from the old-established town of Macon, Georgia, to the new settlement of St Paul, Minnesota, he noted that each had a population of 10 000 and supported three weekly newspapers – but St Paul had four dailies as well. From this he concluded that the size of the local Press in any community was less a function of its total population than it was of the level of its 'general activity'.

Henry King, who founded newspapers in Illinois, Kansas and Missouri, credited the press with being not a by-product of pioneering, but in many cases its very cause. Conceding that sceptics thought 'that the scheme of starting a newspaper before there was any news to print was illogical, fantastic, preposterous', he pointed out that throughout the frontier that was in fact just what had happened: 'The printing press preceded all the usual agencies of society. It did not wait for the rudimentary clutter of things to be composed and organised. The spirit of adventure thrust it forward ahead of the calaboose, the post office, the school, the church, and made it a symbol of conquest.'

When the first issue of *Pittsburgh's Gazette* appeared in 1786, that city had a population of 300. The first editor delivered the newspapers himself within the settlement and persuaded travellers passing through to distribute it in outlying areas. As Pittsburgh flourished so did the *Gazette* – and its editor, who became the postmaster, a bank president, member of the first borough council and one of the founders of its university.

The pioneering issue of Cincinnati's first journal,

MAIL ORDER   Far left: Catalogues offered consumers a far wider choice of high-quality goods than could be stocked by the local general store.
Even large, heavy items such as the kitchen stove (left) could be bought by mail order.

the *Centinel of the North-Western Territory*, was printed in a log cabin and carried a public notice announcing a bounty for 'every scalp, having the right ear appendant, for the first ten Indians' to be killed in the surrounding area. Milwaukee's first newspaper, *The Advertiser*, was established only ten days after Wisconsin Territory had officially come into existence and two months before any land went on sale at Milwaukee itself. The editor, Daniel H. Richards, reckoned that 'the whole population within a circuit of 50 miles (80 km), probably, did not at the time amount to two hundred'. With the enthusiastic support of a real-estate promoter, Richards circulated his paper primarily in the communities from which the future population of Milwaukee was expected to come. The *Kansas Weekly Herald* was produced under the shade of an elm tree, when Leavenworth consisted of a mere four tents. Only five months later, it claimed a circulation of just under 3000. Infant newspapers faced two problems – to get news and to attract readers. While they were waiting for both to accumulate, most received a vital, if indirect, state subsidy from homesteaders. In order to fulfil the required conditions of residence and secure their titles, homesteaders needed to insert an official notice to that effect six times in the newspaper published nearest to their claim. As the charge for such publicity was anything from six to ten dollars, publishers could rely on a good flow of income while they were gradually building

PROMISE OF PLENTY This South Dakota poster of 1890 was designed to tempt immigrants with offers of free homes and land. Uncle Sam is flanked by stereotypes of the most desired migrants – an Englishman and a German.

up their circulation. However, although farm produce was abundant, cash was not, and editors often had to be prepared to accept payment for advertisements in corn, potatoes, molasses or kindling. One desperate soul announced his willingness to accept anything except babies. Despite such financial flexibility, many ventures foundered soon after birth. In 1858 in Nebraska alone six newspapers failed.

Frontier newspapers started before they had readers – and hotels were built before there were any guests to stay in them. As the novelist Anthony Trollope noted in the 1860s: '... the first sign of an incipient settlement is an hotel five storeys high with ... two hundred bedrooms ... When the new hotel rises up in the wilderness, it is presumed that people will come there with the express object of inhabiting it. The hotel itself will create a population. ...'

Memphis boasted such an establishment, surrounded by forest, three years before it was incorporated as a city and ten years before the railroad arrived there. In 1833 Chicago had a population of 350; two years later it acquired its first brick hotel. Within 20 years it had 150 hotels, boarding a sixth of the city's entire population.

The 'American Plan' system provided them with both bed and board, charging for meals whether they were taken or not. Guests ate together in a common dining room and often at a single table. The lack of privacy and enforced informality unsettled fastidious English visitors by blurring their

GOLDEN PROMISES San Francisco (above) mushroomed after the gold rush in the middle of the 19th century. The prospect of making money from big spenders made the city a magnet for prostitutes (right).

accustomed notions of the boundaries between public and private space. In the land of the free it was seldom possible to be free of others. Some hotels would grudgingly provide a meal in one's own room – for a charge. Many refused outright.

Trollope finally conceded that the hotel-as-residence did have some logic to it that was peculiar to the conditions of the West: 'Men there are not fixed in their employment as they are with us . . . Aminadab Wiggs takes an engagement as a clerk at a steamboat office on the Pongowonga river, but he goes to his employment with an inward conviction that six months will see him earning his bread elsewhere. Under such circumstances even a large wardrobe is a nuisance, and a collection of furniture would be as appropriate as a drove of elephants.'

SEATS OF LEARNING

Where virtually every settlement aggrandised its claim to greatness by boasting the title of 'city', one sure way to validate the claim to such status was to have an institution of higher learning. Sectarian rivalry ensured that each Protestant persuasion attempted to found at least one college in each new state or territory. There was vigorous competition between rival communities for the honour of hosting a college, outbidding each other with offers of land and cash. In 1839, six counties battled to become home of the University of Missouri. The winner raised $82 381 in cash and $35 540 in land. Rich and poor alike were involved. Contributions were made by over 900 individuals, of whom only just under ten gave a mere $5 or less. However, the donors' motives were often more down-to-earth than high-minded, as the *Republican* of Wooster, Ohio, revealed when the Presbyterians decided to locate a college in any county that could raise $100 000 towards the building of the project: 'It will not only be an honour to the place but it will so enhance the value of real estate throughout the whole vicinity and county that none will be losers by the investment. . . . '

Canada, though more sparsely populated, also linked educational status and municipal ambition.

A Presbyterian college was founded at Winnipeg in 1871 after its collection of shacks had been incorporated as a city. Four years later, it became home to western Canada's first fully fledged university.

By 1870, 11 colleges had been founded in Kentucky, 13 in Iowa and 21 in Illinois. A decade later, the President of Columbia University wondered how England managed to get by with only four degree-granting institutions when Ohio had 37. As with newspapers, their rate of mortality was high – 80 per cent of colleges established in the west and south-west failed.

Communities that were unable to attract a college often redirected their efforts and lobbied to become the county seat or, failing that, the location of a land office, prison or institution for the blind, deaf or insane. In most cases, what was at stake was a vision of the future rather than a firm stake in the present. The three contestants for the Harlan County seat in Nebraska were Melrose, Republican City and Alma: the first two each consisted of a store and a hitching post; the third was a site marked by a buffalo skull.

ADAPTATION   A Native American Crow family enjoys a meal in totally Europeanised surroundings in 1910 Montana. High-quality tableware is displayed with evident pride, but traditional costume is still worn.

In Canada the transformation of the prairie was even more rapid than in the US. In the 1850s Chief Peguis lamented that: 'Before you whites came to disturb the ground, our rivers were full of fish and woods of deer. Our creeks abounded with beavers and our plains were covered with buffalo. But now we are brought to poverty. We are left to starve while you whites are growing rich on the very dust of our fathers, troubling the plains with the plough, covering them with cows in the summer and in the winter feeding your cattle with hay from the very swamps from which our beavers have been driven.'

NORTH OF THE BORDER

The Reverend William Duncan's first encounter with the Tsimshian Indians of coastal British Columbia confirmed everything he had heard about their debauchery, drunkenness and violence. Worse still, he had even witnessed 'a poor slave woman being murdered in cold blood, thrown on the beach and eaten by two naked savages'. Duncan had his work cut out as first a missionary and then a teacher to the Tsimshian. To protect the tribe from the whiskey peddlers who inhabited his base at Fort Simpson, Duncan resettled the tribe at the abandoned village of Metlakatla, a short distance away. A second settlement was founded 25 years later at New Metlakatla, on Annette Island

First City The port of New Westminster was named at Queen Victoria's suggestion – but was called Stumpville by its inhabitants. It was incorporated as British Columbia's first city in 1860 and served as the provincial capital until 1866.

in Alaska. Under Duncan's guidance, the Tsimshians mastered spinning, soap-making, blacksmithing, carpentry and ran their own salmon cannery, sawmill, baseball team and brass band.

However, the main resistance to settlement came not from the native peoples but from the métis, the mixed-blood descendants of Indian women and those French-Canadian *voyageurs*, who had acted as intermediaries between native hunters and Scottish traders in the lucrative fur trade, but who had then turned to buffalo hunting. An armed rising in 1869-70 won them an award of lands, which was lost in the following decade, due to the hostility and harassment of incoming settlers,

troops and officials. Most of the 10 000 métis headed farther west and, having failed again to secure land rights from the government, took up arms once more in 1885, only to be crushed and dispersed as before.

A champion of the métis cause was Gabriel Dumont, the son of a métis hunter and grandson of a French-Canadian *voyageur*. He took part in his first battle at the age of 13, when he helped to defend a métis encampment against a large Sioux war party. As good a shot with the bow as with the rifle,

Cannibalism to Capitalism English preacher William Duncan (below left) was an eyewitness to cannibalism when he arrived among the Tsimshians of British Columbia in 1857 (below right). Duncan founded two model settlements where the Tsimshians prospered.

headquarters, Dumont evaded capture and fled to the US. Following Riel's execution Dumont joined Buffalo Bill's Wild West Show as a crack marksman, returning to Canada in 1888 after the proclamation of an amnesty. His last years were spent hunting, trading and dictating his vivid memoirs.

Following American precedent, the Dominion Lands Act of 1872 offered homesteads of 160 acres (65 ha) each for a nominal $10 to settlers who were prepared to break, cultivate and live on the land for a period of three years. This was to prove to be a harsh experience for many.

This effective settlement of the Canadian west waited on the completion of transcontinental links and the building of a network of spur lines. Another prerequisite was the establishment of the 'Mounties' to guarantee a minimum of order and to police the border against aggressive American hunters and whiskey drummers. Scarlet-coated to distinguish them from the

Dumont was a superb hunter, horseman and canoeist, and an unrivalled guide. Although illiterate, he spoke six languages and at the age of 25 was elected permanent chief and buffalo hunt leader of the métis on the Saskatchewan river. He negotiated a treaty with the Sioux, and later one with the Blackfoot, and it was these two treaties that subsequently ensured the peaceful penetration of the Canadian prairies.

But Dumont realised that the buffalo herds would soon vanish and that Canadian overlordship was inevitable, so he turned his efforts to asserting the rights of his people to own land for farming. In 1873 he became president of a commune at St Laurent, the first local government to be established between the Rockies and Manitoba. The arrival of the Mounties in 1875 extinguished the commune but Dumont kept up his campaign for métis land rights.

Negotiations proved fruitless, however, and Dumont threw in his lot with the leader of the métis rebels, Louis Riel. During the second métis rebellion of 1885, Dumont proved to be a highly effective guerrilla fighter. After the fall of the métis

CRACKSHOT REBEL Gabriel Dumont was the leader of the failed 1885 uprising of the métis of the Canadian prairies. He fled to the US and appeared in Buffalo Bill's Wild West Show. He returned to Canada after receiving an amnesty.

A MOUNTIE: DUTY DRESSED IN SCARLET

SERGEANT STEELE, erect and purposeful, strode slowly along the boardwalk, nodding and murmuring a greeting to all he knew and making a mental note of the face, dress and mount of those he did not.

As the commander of a small Mountie post, he consciously tried to train his two younger colleagues as much by example as by command. He called his morning stroll 'showing the flag' and only the most urgent business would make him forego it. The scarlet tunic was an instant reassurance to the law-abiding and a constant reminder to those who were not. In a town which was still more of a transit camp than a community, Sam Steele stood for reliability and routine – in a word, for order.

Today he would pause for coffee in the general store; yesterday it was the saloon; tomorrow it would be the railway depot. The counter clerk, the bar keeper and the ticket taker were his eyes and ears, and time spent in their company was seldom wasted. Steele never tried to meet trouble half way but he liked to know well in advance when it was coming. He was one of just 500 red-coated men with responsibility for policing a wilderness five times the size of Great Britain. 'A Mountie is never off duty' was more than his own private motto: it was an essential principle of action.

Returning to his post, Steele paused to check his pocket watch

against the ticking of the London-made wall clock, then, ignoring the snores of the drunk in the cell, set about composing his weekly report.

Although he found paperwork irksome, there was much satisfaction in chronicling the progress of the raw settlement placed in his charge. Steele was not only its policeman but also its customs officer, registrar, medical superintendent and much else besides. There was no bank as yet, so the Mountie post's own safe often held a small fortune in gold dust and cash, not to mention legal documents, all of which had to be listed and accounted for. But there was now a school and a church, and Steele was a dutiful attender at the evening meetings of their committees.

As the light began to fade, Steele was grateful to hear the approach of his deputy, Lockhart, whose own doings could now be added to the weekly report. Lockhart was leading a bedraggled traveller he had found lost along the way. After pointing out a rooming house, he entered the post, saluted and made his report – a broken leg out at the Aikens' place but nothing tricky (he had splinted it himself); a telegraph wire down at the landing stage but the boys should have it fixed by nightfall; an invitation to a wedding at the Presbyterian chapel over by Duck Lake next month. 'Nothin' too excitin',' Lockhart concluded. 'OK, Dave,' grunted Steele, his steel nib pen scratching as he turned up the lamp. 'Let's keep it that way.'

GETTING THEIR MAN
Mounties' uniforms and equipment show their military origins. The first column to penetrate the North-west was armed with artillery, sabres and carbines.

THE LAST WAVE Immigration into western Canada boomed at the turn of the century, encouraged by appeals such as this (right). Many came from Britain, where during 1911-13 emigrants to a new life numbered 400 000.

hated US cavalry, the mounties were welcomed unreservedly by Crowfoot, paramount chief of the Blackfoot confederacy: 'If the police had not come to the country, where would we all be now? Bad men and whiskey were killing us so fast that very few, indeed, of us would have been left today. The police have protected us as the feathers of a bird protect it from the frosts of the winter.' This did not, however, prevent Crowfoot's own son from taking advantage of the 1885 métis rebellion to sack the town of Battleford at the head of a force of 200 warriors, costing the lives of perhaps 80 métis and Indians, and the same number of whites. But in the same month that Louis Riel, the leader of the métis, was executed, the Canadian Pacific Railway was completed, binding west to east with a single, shining band of steel.

POPULATING THE PRAIRIES

The populating of the prairies followed swiftly after the completion of the transcontinental railroad, reaching its peak in the first decade of the 20th century, when Canada welcomed 400 000 immigrants every year. What the Canadian government was looking for was a 'stalwart peasant in a sheepskin coat, born on the soil, whose forefathers have been farmers for ten generations, with a stout wife and a half dozen children'.

There were thousands of immigrants like this, from Germany, the Netherlands, Scandinavia and the Ukraine. But there were also Jews fleeing Russian persecution, Polish miners, fishermen from Canada's own maritime provinces, Americans of all sorts from across the border, and thousands of English city dwellers, totally unprepared for life on the plains. As ever with frontier settlers, those who could best endure the hardships with fortitude, endurance and endeavour were the ones who survived and flourished.

69

THE LANDS OF GREAT ESTATES

Unlike the United States, where homesteading farmers outnumbered cowboys by

a thousand to one, the virgin lands of Argentina and Brazil were usually

exploited as immense ranches and plantations.

SOUTH AMERICAN Indians practised terraced farming in the well-watered valleys of the north-western interior of Argentina long before the Spanish invaders trickled over the mountains from Peru and Chile in the late 1500s to establish a chain of forts. These forts, which eventually grew into cities such as Tucuman, Jujuy and Córdoba, became settlements and supplied food and livestock to arid but silver-rich Bolivia. As the mines there became exhausted, Argentina's growth region came to focus around the expanding port of Buenos Aires to the south-east. A trade route linked the north-west and south-east, skirting the broad, treeless *pampas* (prairies) to the south with its fierce population of Indian hunters. The regions to the north-east of the route, known as Gran Chaco and Mesopotamia, proved equally difficult to penetrate because of the harsh environment and the fierce resistance of the Indians.

Estancias (large cattle estates) were established north-west of Buenos Aires in the late 1600s but settlement remained sparse. As late as 1810, the population of Argentina was less than half a million. Of those, perhaps as many as a third were Indians and another 10 per cent black or mulatto slaves or ex-slaves of African descent.

The European settlement of Brazil began in the late 1500s when the Portuguese established the

continued on page 73

TRAVELLERS' REST The South American *gauchos*, or cowboys, carried their goods across the prairies in high-wheeled carts. Traditional dress, as shown in this painting of the 1820s, included striped ponchos.

OPENING A CONTINENT The railways and new crops such as rubber helped to bring new opportunities for South America's pioneers.

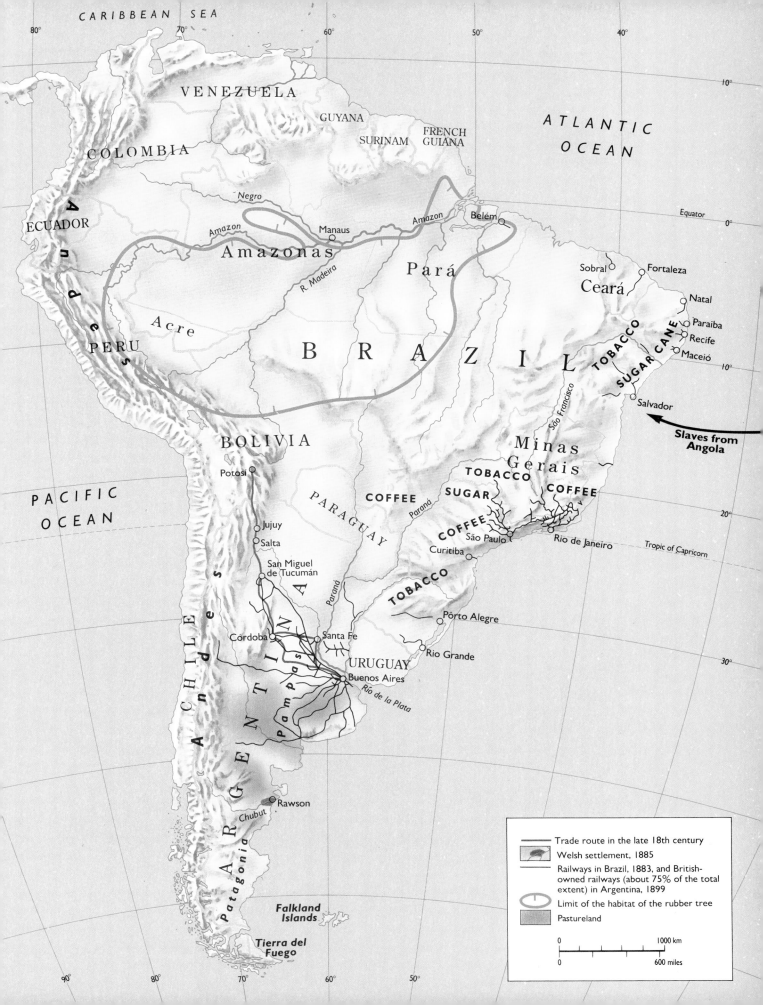

CARIBBEAN SEA

80° 70° 60° 50° 40°

ATLANTIC
OCEAN

VENEZUELA

GUYANA

COLOMBIA

SURINAM

FRENCH
GUIANA

10°

ECUADOR

Negro

Equator 0°

Amazon

Manaus

Amazon

Belém

Sobral Fortaleza

Andes

Amazonas

Pará

Ceará

Natal

PERU

R. Madeira

Acre

BRAZIL

TOBACCO

Paraíba
Recife
Maceió

10°

SUGAR CANE

Salvador

Slaves from
Angola

PACIFIC
OCEAN

BOLIVIA

Potosí

São Francisco

Minas
Gerais

COFFEE

TOBACCO

SUGAR

Jujuy

PARAGUAY

COFFEE

COFFEE

Salta

Paraná

São Paulo

Rio de Janeiro

Tropic of Capricorn

20°

San Miguel
de Tucumán

Curitiba

Andes

TOBACCO

Córdoba

ARGENTINA

Paraná

Santa Fe

Pôrto Alegre

Rio Grande

30°

Pampas

URUGUAY

Buenos Aires

Río de la Plata

Rawson

Chubut

Patagonia

Falkland
Islands

Tierra del
Fuego

90° 80° 70° 60° 50°

Trade route in the late 18th century
Welsh settlement, 1885
Railways in Brazil, 1883, and British-
owned railways (about 75% of the total
extent) in Argentina, 1899
Limit of the habitat of the rubber tree
Pastureland

0 1000 km

0 600 miles

A GAUCHO: ONLY THE COWS FOR COMPANY

HE ROSE BEFORE DAWN, murmuring the motto of his foreman like a prayer to the saints: 'A *puestero* who does not get up early is no good at all.' Promoted to take charge of a *puesto* (post) at the centre of a well-watered *rodeo* (pasture) on a remote part of the Estancia San Isabel, Ramon Ramírez was accustomed to working alone for a week at a time between visits from his boss.

The puesto was new and consisted of the bare minimum: a *rancho* of mud and branches with a thatched roof where he ate, slept and stored his few possessions; and a *ramada* – four poles with a roof of branches, where he stabled his horses and took his afternoon siesta in a hammock. His furnishings were crude – a hide bed, a cooking-pot and an iron kettle for maté. There was no bench, no table and no oven, and the skull of a steer served as a stool. In the cold dawn Ramon sipped bitter maté. He would not eat until the sun was high; then, after devouring a thick hunk of roast beef, he would rest.

Most of the day he rode the circuit of his rodeo, checking for the tracks of strays. Occasionally he would find one which had wandered into a wooded *arroyo* or gully, lasso the stray and lead it back to the herd.

Branding was another task which had to be done throughout the year. As a branding mark was proof of ownership, the puestero who wielded the iron was a man in a position of trust. A lost or stolen iron would cost him his job; making a new one required a police permit.

Castration was usually done at the same time as branding. Only a fifth of the healthiest young bulls were saved for breeding. Every day as Ramon inspected his animals, he would make a mental note of the fattest, destined to become steers and be slaughtered. Any diseased beast he would drive far away from the rest, then kill it to prevent infection spreading, burning the carcass and burying the ashes.

After his siesta, he would round up the herd of a thousand cattle and pen them in the wooden corrals beside the rancho. At sundown he kept out the cold with a cup of *caña* – sugar-cane brandy – and sat beside his fire, stirring his supper of *locro* – corn boiled in water with grease and salt.

Ramon was looking forward to next month when they would all join together to celebrate the fiesta of San Isidoro, the local patron saint, and to the eight days of singing, dancing, guitars, horse races, cards and cockfights.

DRYING THE HIDES Men peg out the scraped hides to dry in the fierce sun, while a poncho-clad rider gallops past.

NOBLE SAVAGES   In this romantic depiction of the Indians of the pampas, it is worth noting the ingenious folding-frame shelters and the central figure, who is about to cast a bola – three stones on a rope – in order to catch his horse.

world's first large sugar-cane plantations around Bahia and Pernambuco, worked by African slave labour. The south-east was settled in the 1700s after the discovery of gold and diamonds. Rio de Janeiro prospered as the outport for this mining region. All other regions have been developed since their independence in the 1820s. By that time, the hunter-gatherer Indian population had been driven into the forests, a substantial black population had been imported from Africa and the white population was still primarily of Portuguese descent.

FORWARD INTO THE PAMPAS

The exploitation of the pampas – an area south-east of Buenos Aires, and three times the size of France – began in the 17th century with the organisation of *vaquerías*, hunting expeditions to prey on the wild cattle that roamed the prairies. The vaquerías were organised by Spanish-descended settlers granted land by the Crown. The cattle hides were stripped off and staked out to dry in the sun. The fat was boiled to make tallow, and the tongue – the tastiest and tenderest part – was used for food. Most of the remaining meat was left to rot in the sun or

FACE OF THE FUTURE   The billowing smokestacks of the salting house and the ships in the background show the impact that technology and trade had on traditional Argentine life.

feed the vultures, with wild dogs circling at a prudent distance.

Over the following two centuries, overseas demand for the products of the prairie lands expanded hugely with the industrialisation of Britain and then the United States. Leather was needed for footwear, saddlery, upholstery, book-bindings, buckets, hats and aprons, as well as for the component parts of carriages and ships' rigging. By the 1850s, Britain was importing half a million Argentine hides through Liverpool alone.

The now-mechanised British and North American woollen cloth industry looked abroad to meet their vastly expanding needs. Argentine wool was cheap, dirty, greasy and coarse, but by interbreeding native sheep with French Merinos and British Southdowns, Cheviots and Leicesters, the fleeces became finer and weighed twice as much. After the conquest of Patagonia in the 1870s, immigrant Welsh shep-herds brought with them invaluable expertise in sheep rearing.

ESTABLISHING THE ESTANCIAS

As the wild herds of cattle dwindled, hunting was seen to be wasteful and inefficient. Estancias were established, where branded cattle could be grazed on designated but fenceless pastures, called rodeos. Gauchos – roughly one man for every 1000 head of cattle – were now needed for round-ups, branding, slaughtering, breaking saddle-horses, building

wooden corrals and, in the early days, flaying hides. A dried hide was worth more than the live animal, but producing it required considerable labour. A German Jesuit in the 18th century noted that the hides are: '. . . carefully fastened to the ground, to be dried, with wooden pegs, under shelter, in a place where the fresh air is admitted; and lest moths should gnaw or strip them of their hairs, for 13, or at least eight days, the dust which engenders these insects must be diligently beaten from them with a stick. This labour, which was often continued for many months, whilst some thousands of them were disposed of, is rated very high. . . .'

Cattle-ranching began to spread out onto the pampas. The export of dried, salted beef as a food for Cuban slaves, Spanish soldiers and British sailors opened up a new and profitable market for what had formerly been discarded as waste, further encouraging the estancia movement. Many estates were enormous, averaging 100-200 sq miles (260-518 sq km). Even larger estancias supported up to 600 people. A large central ranch on the estancia would often have its own general store, chapel, limekilns, workshops for turning tallow into soap or candles, and housing for casual labourers. These were taken on as extra hands at the busiest times of the year: slaughtering in the summer, from December until March, when the weather was ideal for drying hides and meat; and wood-cutting in the southern winter, between June and August. The hired hands might be paid in silver pesos or in goods from the store, such as tobacco, shirts and bridles.

The Greening of the Pampas

As the expanding market for farming products pushed the frontier of exploitation ever farther into the unsettled southern prairies, Argentine farming became organised in a series of recognisable belts. Farmers within reach of Buenos Aires' markets – a distance of roughly 60 miles (100 km) – raised grain, fruit, vegetables, poultry and dairy animals. Farming methods were crude, but the fertility of the virgin soil compensated for their ignorance of crop rotation and their failure to manure. They

FRONTIER ENTERTAINMENT An organ-grinder amuses a group of gauchos with his performing monkey. The proprietor of the *pulpería* looks on from behind the security of an iron grating. Below: Races were rough – knocking a rival off his mount was considered a fair tactic.

THE WELSH INVASION

The Welsh began the settlement of Patagonia, at the southern end of the South American continent, and there are still Welsh-speaking communities there today. Some 3000 immigrants settled in the area from 1865 to 1915. Their self-governing, chapel-based communities gave the vote to both men and women, organised cooperatives to sell members' crops, ran non-profit-making shops, and provided credit and medical insurance.

WELSH SETTLERS The isolation of this early Patagonian farm belies the strength of the communities created by Welsh immigrants. Their hold over local government and education was resented – and broken down by government pressure in favour of Spanish-speakers.

used ox bones for ploughshares, and threshing was done by driving horses back and forth for hours to trample the grain the farmers had hand-harvested. The grain was then stored in oxhide sacks suspended from poles to keep it from rats. Grasslands midway between the port and frontier were given over to sheep, while cattle-grazing dominated the distant hinterlands.

Hot summers, mild winters and plentiful rain made the most natural pastures of the pampas well worth exploiting. Europeans had already changed its ecology by planting shade trees around their settlements and introducing not only horses and cattle, but also – accidentally – rats and dogs, which multiplied rapidly and became ferocious predators. The growth of ranching enriched the soil with manure, converting coarse grasses into lush pasture. Left to itself, this greening process took about 30 years; but the deliberate sowing of rich lucernes could accomplish this in just a couple of seasons. The land was further 'sweetened' by man-made fires which burned off tall, tough weeds. In time, the wildlife also changed as ostriches, antelope and armadillos were pushed south with the Indians.

Indian raids were punished by savage reprisals. In the 1830s Charles Darwin, during the course of his voyage around the world in the *Beagle*, expressed his revulsion at the routine killing of Indian women of childbearing age. A

gaucho simply shrugged and replied: 'Why, what can be done? They breed so!' As late as 1876, Indians raided to within 200 miles (320 km) of Buenos Aires, carrying off 500 white captives and 300 000 head of cattle. A one-sided and genocidal 'Desert Campaign' in 1879-85 pitched Argentine regulars, armed with repeating rifles, against Indians, armed with lances, resulting in the elimination of the so-called 'Indian menace'.

Ranchers paid their men bounties for killing dogs and pumas, as well as Indians. Prairie dogs, whose earthen tunnels undermined pastures, were destroyed by suffocating them in their burrows with sulphur smoke.

BATTLING WITH THE ELEMENTS

Drought, however, remained the real terror, killing livestock by the thousand and bankrupting their owners. It also decimated the wild herds on which Indians relied for their meat, forcing them to raid frontier ranches for food. Even field mice, deprived of natural vegetation, were driven to devour fields of grain. Throughout the century the drought cycle, which occurred roughly every 10-15 years, remained closely correlated with economic catastrophe, civil disorder, frontier fighting and massive increases in imports of flour.

RAIL ROUTES Railroads played a vital part in opening up Latin America's hinterland. By 1914 there were 21 800 miles (34 880 km) of track in Argentina and 15 445 miles (24 712 km) in Brazil.

Whereas most cowboys were paid in cash or kind, shepherds were often rewarded by a system of profit-sharing. This enabled them to keep as much sheep meat as they wanted, plus a third of the annual increase over the previous year in wool, skins and tallow. On the unfenced prairie, profit-sharing was justified on the grounds that on land where a paddock system was impossible, the shepherd who tended his flock on a profit-share would do his work more thoroughly and conscientiously than a hireling.

WORKERS OF THE LAND

The best shepherds proved to be Basques, political refugees from Spain's civil wars, and Irishmen, economic refugees from the devastating potato famine of the 1840s. Many took advantage of the profit-sharing system to build up sizable herds of their own, some becoming modest landowners and avoiding the normal fate of immigrant farmers, who became tenants, sharecroppers or paid employees on a large estancia. From the 1840s onwards, each small town in the sheep belt had a *grasería* – a steam-powered plant for boiling down grease and tallow from the wool. Shearing was done from October to December, with the help of hired gangs who were paid a piece rate, plus meals, shelter and *yerba* – a tea made from the leaves of the Paraguayan yerba tree which contained both

EUROPEAN INFLUENCES The costume of this Argentine gentleman combines European elegance with frontier romance. Below: A windpump towers above a typical estancia house on the Argentine prairies.

caffeine and tannin. Despite the shortage of labour relative to the size of the land, the landowner was usually at an advantage, as the law stated that any *peón* (labourer) unable to prove employment, would be considered a vagabond and liable to army conscription or forced labour on public works. Peóns seeking to change employers were required to show a note of release and good behaviour from their previous boss. Remote from alternative employment, sons followed fathers to work for the same estancia.

Social and economic life in the countryside revolved around *pulperías* (taverns) and *tiendas* (rural stores). A census of 1858 showed that in the province of Buenos Aires alone, there were 1100 pulperías and 280 tiendas – a ratio of one tavern or store for every 75 inhabitants. Here, country folk bought tobacco, strong spirits, yerba, hardware, salt and knick-knacks, often paying with hides,

IDLE RICH The wives of the wealthy spent their days doing very little. Unoccupied by knitting or reading, they stare vacantly from their iron-barred seclusion, watching life pass by.

fleeces or farm produce. Outside, the shade of an Andean ombu tree provided a gathering place for gossip, card-playing and spontaneous singing and dancing. The larger pulperías and tiendas on main roads were where craftsmen could be found, as well as a reserve pool of female and child labour to draw upon for seasonal work.

Although the population of Argentina more than tripled in the first half of the 19th century, in 1859 it stood at around 10 million and the area under cultivation was no bigger than the island of Malta. Forty years of warlord rivalry in the provinces had reduced many parts of the interior to poverty. As late as 1869, four-fifths of the population were illiterate.

EYEWITNESS

OBSERVATIONS ON A DEVELOPING NATION

WHEN CAPTAIN Francis Bond Head retired from the British army in 1825, he accepted a post as supervisor of an Andean mine. He was deeply impressed by the immensity of the pampas and an ardent admirer of the gaucho as a sort of noble savage. The female of the species, however, held far less appeal for him:

6 The habits of the women are very curious; they have literally nothing to do; the great plains which surround them offer them no motive to walk, they seldom ride, and their lives certainly are very indolent and inactive. They have all, however, families, whether married or not; and once when I enquired of a young woman employed in nursing a very pretty child, who was the father of the *creatura* [creature] she replied: "Who knows?" '

High society fared little better in Captain Head's estimation:

'Some of the principal families of Buenos Aires furnish their rooms in a very expensive but comfortless manner. . . They get an English pianoforte, and some marble vases, but they have no idea of grouping their furniture into a comfortable form; the ladies sit with their backs against the walls . . . and when a stranger calls upon them, he is much surprised to find that they have the uncourteous custom of never rising from their chairs! 9

BROAD BOULEVARDS Inspired by the street plans of the French capital, the impressive thoroughfares, lined with ponderous apartment blocks, supported Buenos Aires' claim to be the 'Paris of the South'. The photograph was taken in the early years of this century. Left: Thousands of immigrants eked out a precarious living as street vendors or entertainers.

In 1854 the future arrived – with the country's first six-mile stretch of railway. By 1914, Argentina had the tenth largest railway network in the world.

For centuries, the journey between two of its greatest provincial cities, Rosario and Córdoba, had taken a month by ox cart. It now took two days by rail. Further tools of modern technology, effecting similar transformations in the Argentine pampas, included barbed wire, the wind-pump, the repeating rifle, the mechanical mower and the refrigerator-ship.

As early as the 1860s, sheep-farming surpassed cattle products as the nation's largest export earner and by the 1880s, Argentina had 30 sheep for every man, woman and child in the country. In that same decade, foreign trade increased in value by two-and-a-half times, the advent of steel-hulled cargo vessels powered by steam turbines halving freight rates between 1877 and 1886. By the early 1880s, flour overtook fleeces as the nation's number one earner. By 1914 the two most advanced regions of what had become one of the ten richest countries in the world were the areas around Buenos Aires and the pampas. In just half a century, they had been conquered and tamed, while the ancient cities of the interior slumbered in provincial stagnation.

In the wake of this development came an avalanche of immigrants, more than 3 million between 1871 and 1914. The Italians were the most numerous, followed by the Spanish, Poles and Russians. But there were also British and Austro-Hungarians, and even 80 000 'Turcos' – Turks, Syrians and Lebanese. In little more than 50 years, over a 100 immigrant settlements were founded.

PARIS OF THE SOUTH

The paradox of Argentina's success was that a national economy founded on fleece, flour, hides and beef gave birth to a city so dazzling that it made the breathtaking grandeur of the pampas seem dull by comparison.

Buenos Aires originally prospered on slavery, smuggling and silver. By 1776, when it was designated as the capital of La Plata, the port had a population of just over 20 000, still only about half that of inland Córdoba, then the largest city south of Lima. Fifty years later, Buenos Aires had doubled its population. In 1825 a British soldier, Francis Head, found that it was: 'Far from being an agreeable residence

. . . badly paved and dirty . . . The walls, from the climate, are damp, mouldy and discoloured . . . The roofs have no ceilings and the families have no ideas of warming themselves, except by drinking hot maté or by huddling round a fire of charcoal.'

In the 1820s, Sir Woodbine Parish, Britain's first diplomatic representative, dismissed it as a 'disagreeable and disheartening place', surrounded by a 'land of mud and putrid carcasses'. But even the most pompous of visitors had to concede that the *porteños* – the people of Buenos Aires – had a certain style, and were astonished to find that beggars plied their trade on horseback. They also ate well – consuming an average of 500 lb (227 kg) of beef per person per year.

LIFE IN THE CAPITAL

By the mid century, Buenos Aires was still little more than a cluster of villages linked by dirt roads, with a mortality rate twice as high as that of contemporary London. In 1871 alone, 7000 people died in a yellow fever epidemic. Then, over the next 40 years, the city was transformed as the British built the docks, waterworks and gasworks, and laid the drains and tramways. The Germans installed electricity and the Italians built mansions and broad boulevards in the opulent French Beaux Arts style.

The glory of the city and the focus of its glittering social scene was the Teatro Colón, the largest opera house in the world. On the outskirts were built cool, exclusive suburbs such as Temperley and Hurlingham, where the wealthy spoke English in their mock-Gothic mansions, played polo, tennis and rugby and sent their sons to British-style boarding schools. As the main port of reception for

GENTLEMEN INVADERS   European settlers maintained their Old World standards of dress and lifestyle. Many of the wealthy settlers copied the British way of life, admiring greatly their solid Victorian values and their spirit of endeavour.

immigrants, the city became intensely cosmopolitan: a South American New York, half of whose inhabitants were foreign-born. By the first decade of the 20th century Buenos Aires, with a

SPECIMENS OF HUMANITY   From 1783 to 1792, an expedition of Portuguese scholar-explorers travelled 25 000 miles (40 000 km) along Brazil's waterways, recording with precision the native peoples they encountered.

A NATURALIST OVERWHELMED BY NATURE

WHEN CHARLES DARWIN accompanied HMS *Beagle* on its voyage round the world in 1832-6, he landed at the Brazilian port of Bahia. Although the area had been settled for almost three centuries, the richness and splendour of the surrounding countryside still moved him to wonder:

❝ The land is one great wild, untidy luxuriant hothouse, made by nature for herself . . . How great would be the desire in every admirer of nature to behold the scenery of another planet! Yet, to every person in Europe, it may be truly said, that at the distance of only a few degrees from his native soil, the glories of another world are opened to him . . . Delight itself . . . is a weak term to express the feelings of a naturalist who, for the first time, has wandered by himself in a Brazilian forest. The elegance of the grasses, the novelty of the parasitical plants, the beauty of the flowers, the glossy green of the foliage, but above all the general luxuriance of the vegetation, filled me with admiration. A most paradoxical mixture of sound and silence pervades the shady parts of the wood. The noise from the insects is so loud that it may be heard even in a vessel anchored several hundred yards from the shore; yet within the recesses of the forest a universal silence appears to reign . . . In England any person . . . enjoys in his walks a great advantage, by always having something to attract his attention; but in these fertile climates, teeming with life, the attractions are so numerous, that he is scarcely able to walk at all. ❞

WORLD VOYAGE **During the voyage of the *Beagle* the natural world of Brazil was identified and recorded.**

THE DANGERS OF DRINK

In the early 19th century, Buenos Aires had 600 *pulperías* (taverns) selling local wine and brandies and imported rum, beer and 'square face' – gin. In the 1840s the British Hospital recorded that 70 per cent of deaths were due to alcoholism.

population of 1.5 million, was the largest city in Latin America and home to one-fifth of the entire population of Argentina. As the true gaucho of the plains was fading into memory, so the spirited sounds of the tango filled the night air.

BRAZIL: COFFEE AND CONQUEST

Coffee-growing played a very important part in Brazil's economic success. Slave gangs cleared the forests of trees and tangled undergrowth, so that coffee bush seedlings could be planted in the soft soil in well-spaced rows. As it took three years for the bushes to fruit, they would also sow, between the rows, corn, beans and *macio* – a plant used to make flour. This crop would provide labourers with the bulk of their food and, at the same time, shade the tender coffee bushes from the sun. Although fish and meat were cheap, they rarely formed part of the slaves' diet. Most owners considered that few slaves had more than ten years of useful work in them; it was also cheaper to replace them than to worry about their welfare.

Coffee was only one of a succession of resources which dominated the economic life of Brazil. The first was *brasa* – a red wood used in the 16th century for dyeing – from which the country gets

STATUS SYMBOL **The slave-borne sedan chair, taking this rich lady on a visit, not only signified wealth but also protected her fine clothes from the dirty streets.**

BOTANICAL BARRIER **Travelling by river was the only way of getting through the rain forest (left). The eventual arrival of roads threatened the very landscape they had penetrated.**

A RUBBER TAPPER: BLEEDING THE LATEX FOREST

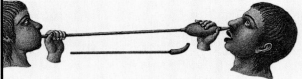

DRUGGED DREAMS
Amazonian Indians snorted through a syringe that was made from rubber.

HALFWAY THROUGH his morning's work, Affonso da Silva remembered it was Saturday. As a *seringueiro* (rubber tapper), working virtually alone in the forest for up to six months at a stretch, it was easy to lose track of the days. Tomorrow, Sunday, he would trek to the southernmost point of a line of hevea trees, which he tapped on alternate days, and Martim, his partner, would come to the northernmost point of his line. They would meet, say a rosary, share a bottle of sugar-cane brandy and swap whatever they had hunted or gathered to eat. More importantly, each would be reassured to find that the other was not suffering from fever, snakebite or injury. If either failed to make the rendezvous, the other would search for him. They had come to Amazonia four years before, after a drought had driven them from neighbouring farms in Ceara on the north-east coast. Rubber-tapping was the only way they could raise money together; both still had families – somewhere.

Affonso reached his next tree after a ten-minute trudge, and gathered up the blob of raw latex that had gathered near its base. At the end of the day he would return to his hut on the river bank and make a smoky fire of oily nuts and damp wood. He would hold lumps of the latex over this to dry out surplus liquid and then roll it into balls.

REWARDS OF PATIENCE
A rubber tapper had to tap at least a hundred rubber trees in the first four hours of daylight. Then he rolled the coagulated latex into balls of rubber (right).

When his supplies ran out, he knew it would be time to go to the company store and exchange his crop for more food, drink and bullets. There never seemed to be enough left over to pay off more than a fraction of his initial debt for tools, rifle and supplies. He could always run away and work for another company which would probably ask no questions, but he had sworn to stay with Martim. If they parted, would he be able to find another partner he could rely on to make a weekly rendezvous? He had seen many trappers half-mad with solitude and drink. Would he trust such a man to find and care for him if he was sick or hurt? But if he tried to leave the valley, he knew he would be arrested downstream and brought back. The jungle was vast but the ways through it were so few that they could easily be found. No, he had to stay, but Affonso's farm and family, after four years, seemed as far away as ever.

PALACES OF PRIDE Argentina boasted the world's largest opera house and Brazil the world's most remote. Each symbolised its nation's claim to rival Europe in wealth and sophistication.

its name. Next came sugar, which initially entailed importing African slaves to cut and crush the cane, and ultimately led to a cattle industry. Oxen were needed to transport the cut cane from the fields to the mills, and to drive the non-water-powered mills. Oxen were also killed for their meat and to yield hides for sacks, harness, boots and aprons.

Gold and diamonds, discovered in the interior frontier province of Minas Gerais, lured marauding *bandeiras* (gangs) of mixed-race and white renegades into becoming the unwitting pioneers of Brazil's advancing frontier, setting the limits of the country's 9000 miles (14 500 km) of land borders.

The bandeiras were merciless slave-hunters, selling the natives to provide cheap labour. Tobacco was a slave-grown crop, five-sixths of it being processed into snuff for export to Europe. Tobacco was used as payment by the Portuguese-Brazilian slave-traders when they bought prisoners of war for slaves from African chiefs. It was also smoked as a consolation by the slaves themselves.

There were other riches which remained unexploited.

LIQUID GOLD Coffee plantations provided employment for both male and female labour. Coffee exports paid for imports of technology and consumer goods.

The first thorough description of the Upper Amazon, written by a Spanish priest in 1639, recognised it as potentially the world's 'best dispensary of medicines . . . a thousand kinds of herbs and trees of very peculiar qualities'.

FROM COLONY TO NATION

Brazilian independence from Portuguese rule was won in 1822. The slave trade and coffee production continued to expand until, by 1837, Brazil was supplying two-thirds of Europe's coffee. The country's economy was growing, but it was not modernising. The gap between the wealthy and educated elite and the illiterate mass, who had many needs but lacked the money, was enormous.

The modernisation of the Brazilian economy began in mid century, when its 3 million sq miles (7 million sq km) of territory still contained only 7.7 million inhabitants. Almost all of these were living along the eastern seaboard, with few concentrated in cities. Towns, such as they were, still consisted mostly of packed-mud houses and unlit streets. 'Slash-and-burn' was still the standard technique for clearing land for cultivation and 'renewing' pasture. Soil erosion was common and planned fertilisation as unknown as farm machinery. Even sugar-processing techniques were much the same as they had been two centuries before.

The only technical education in the country was limited to a few engineers trained at the military academy; there were no vocational schools. Among the small educated class, a serious interest in science

was limited to after-dinner conversation. The wealthy set aspired to the lifestyle of the British, whom they admired for their self-confidence, legal system, high-quality manufacturing, and prominent mercantile and naval presence. In Brazil, politicians quoted Gladstone in their speeches and sweltered in parliament in top hats and frock coats, because that was how it was done at Westminster. Young men renounced their traditional passions – poetry, politics and prostitutes – for those of soccer and self-improvement.

From the 1850s onwards, the pace of change began to quicken. Provincial revolts against the central government had occurred continuously during the previous 30 years, but the last was suppressed in 1849. That year the slave trade was abolished, though slavery continued. In 1871 the liberal-minded emperor Dom Pedro II proclaimed the Law of the Free Womb – every child born of a slave woman would henceforth be free. In fact, the tide of voluntary liberation was already flowing strongly. In 1887 the army refused orders to hunt down escapees from slavery 'as it was beneath the dignity of officers and gentlemen to employ the national armed forces for such an ignoble purpose'. On May 13, 1888, the 'Golden Law' was promulgated, finally ending two-and-a-half centuries of slavery. There was no

MULTIRACIAL SOCIETY Many Brazilians were descended from former African slaves.

compensation for slave owners, who soon had their revenge when the army toppled the throne within months, inaugurating a republic in 1889. The abolition of the slave trade encouraged immigration by the literate, skilled and enterprising on an unprecedented scale, further assisted by the inauguration of a regular steam packet service between Brazil and Britain in 1851. The result was that 882 176 newcomers arrived between 1850 and 1888.

Steam power was introduced on the rivers, penetrating the vast, unexploited interior and beginning the mechanisation of the cotton industry. Many factories were established for the production of basic goods and railway mileage increased. Most lines led inland from the coast, linking it to ever more remote coffee-growing areas of the frontier, thrusting settlement forward. Much of this growth was chaotic and laggardly; by 1880 the newly built railways were operating on 13 different gauges. But, despite a personal crusade on behalf of education by Dom Pedro II, by 1889 only one school-age child in 15 attended school.

CITY BY THE SEA Rio de Janeiro, situated by one of the most magnificent natural harbours in the world, rapidly grew to be the commercial centre of Brazil.

VAGABONDS AND ADVENTURERS

Australia and New Zealand both shared

a common British heritage and found good fortune through

rich natural resources and a fertile agriculture.

But the divergent nature of their settlers, and the resistance

that they faced, led to the evolution of two

quite distinct societies.

CONVICTS AND SQUATTERS

Matthew Flinders, the first explorer to sail all the way round Australia, called it

'a poor dried-up land afflicted only by fever and flies' – but to generations of newcomers,

voluntary or otherwise, it proved a golden land of plenty.

FIREPOWER Soldiers at the penal settlement of Botany Bay protected newcomers from the Aborigines.

A SETTLER ARRIVING in New South Wales in 1828, just 40 years after the first British penal colony was established there, would have found a society that was already energetically forging its own identity. Fewer than half the population of approximately 5000 colonists were actual convicts, although almost all the rest, apart from the military and officials, were 'emancipists' – people who had served their time and decided to stay on.

Their very use of English testified to a vigorous approach to their destiny. They carefully avoided the word 'convict', referring instead to an 'old hand', a 'Government man' or even a 'pensioner of the Crown'. Their motley brood of offspring, tanned, tough, barefoot and cocksure, were known as 'currency' – a wry comparison between them and the local monetary system, which mixed Indian rupees, Dutch guilders, Irish banknotes, the Commissariat Officer's 'Store Receipts' and Spanish dollars. This medium of exchange bore witness

to the locals' ingenuity, since the British authorities in setting up the colony had failed to provide them with a proper currency. The 'currency' children contrasted with the 'sterling', also known as 'pure Merinos' (after the recently introduced merino sheep), who were free emigrants from Britain. Along with the officers and former officers of a specially formed militia, the New South Wales Corps, these people regarded themselves as the colony's elite.

Far outnumbering the colonists, meanwhile, were Australia's indigenous peoples, the Aborigines, whose ancestors had crossed from Asia and New Guinea on long-vanished land bridges some 50 000 to 30 000 years ago. They lived in scattered groups, numbering anything up to a few million people in all, and spoke more than 200 different languages, some of which had less in common

LAND OF OPPORTUNITIES Australia's 19th-century wealth was built on sheep, cattle and gold.

TRANSPORTATION DISASTER

The voyage of the Second Fleet was one of the most disastrous in the history of transportation. Of 1006 prisoners who sailed from Portsmouth, 267 died at sea and at least another 150 soon after landing in 1790. Many could only crawl ashore or had to be carried. The contractors, former slave-shippers Camden, Calvert and King, were given the contract for the Third Fleet.

FIGHTING MEN
The Aboriginal warriors tried to defend their lands from encroaching European settlers.

than English and Russian. Each tribe's lands were sacred to its people as well as being a source of sustenance. It was hardly surprising that by 1818

encroachments by the new arrivals had already led to conflict. This would persist in intermittent raids and attacks upon each other by colonists and Aborigines alike for decades to come.

The Aborigines also found themselves susceptible to diseases the colonists inadvertently brought

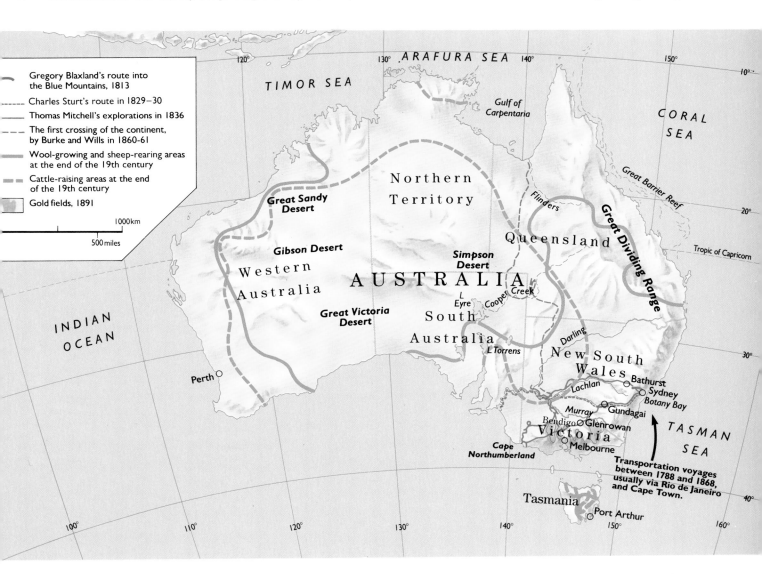

- Gregory Blaxland's route into the Blue Mountains, 1813
- Charles Sturt's route in 1829–30
- Thomas Mitchell's explorations in 1836
- The first crossing of the continent, by Burke and Wills in 1860-61
- Wool-growing and sheep-rearing areas at the end of the 19th century
- Cattle-raising areas at the end of the 19th century
- Gold fields, 1891

1000km
500 miles

TIMOR SEA
ARAFURA SEA
Gulf of Carpentaria
CORAL SEA
Great Barrier Reef
Northern Territory
Great Sandy Desert
Gibson Desert
Western Australia
AUSTRALIA
Simpson Desert
Flinders
Queensland
Great Dividing Range
Tropic of Capricorn
Great Victoria Desert
South Australia
Creek
L Eyre
Cooper
INDIAN OCEAN
L Torrens
Darling
New South Wales
Bathurst
Lachlan
Sydney
Botany Bay
Perth
Murray
Gundagai
Bendigo Glenrowan
TASMAN SEA
Cape Northumberland
Victoria
Melbourne
Transportation voyages between 1788 and 1868, usually via Rio de Janeiro and Cape Town.
Tasmania
Port Arthur

A CONVICT BOUND FOR BOTANY BAY

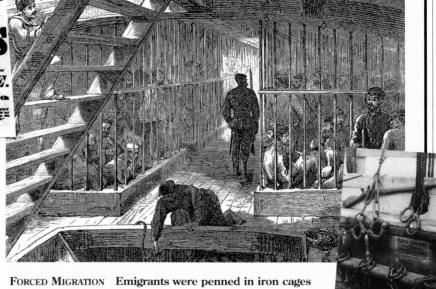

THE SHIP 'NILE'
MORE CONVICTS
IS IN THE HARBOUR.
Remember the LEAGUE.
REMEMBER the Lieutenant-Governor's DESPATCH of the 20th
August, 1847:
GOD Save the QUEEN!

FORCED MIGRATION Emigrants were penned in iron cages under armed guard (above), and clapped in leg manacles weighing 35 lb (16 kg) (right). The 1850 Tasmanian poster (left) declares local opposition to receiving more convicts.

ONLY THE FAINTEST GLIMMER of light through the hatchway told him that it was still day. From the sickening pitch and roll of the ship and the roaring sweep of water across the decks, he knew that they had hit rough seas. There would be no exercise period on deck, no sight of daylight, and no breath of fresh air to relieve the fetid stench compounded of sweat, vomit, urine, excrement and chloride of lime that made him breathe perpetually in short, shallow gasps. His head turned sideways into his bunk, so that he stared sightlessly at the wooden wall of the ship. Today was a day, if not of repentance, then at least of reflection. Now that he had only his own survival to think of, he had to be grateful for conditions as they were.

Twenty years before, things would have been much worse – nowadays, unless the ship sank, the chances were that he would at least get there alive. The system had been going for more than 30 years, and the death rate on the voyage out was down to about one in 100. The contractors – who quoted for transport, food and clothing, at so much per head – received a bonus for every convict landed in good health, and suffered a loss for each one who died. More importantly,

there was a Royal Navy surgeon-superintendent on board, who was answerable not to the contractors but to the British Admiralty, to ensure adequate food and medical care were provided as stipulated.

Today must be Monday, reasoned the convict, because they had been given pork with peas. On Tuesdays and Fridays it was beef and rice, on Wednesdays and Sundays suet pudding, on Thursday the same as Monday, and on Saturday only pork. Each day there was a ration of 2 qts (2 litres) of water and a drink of lime juice, sugar and vinegar to ward off scurvy – the dreaded disease, caused by a lack of vitamin C, whose symptoms included bleeding gums and general debilitation.

They were days out from their last port of call for water and supplies. The ship was hundreds of miles from land and the prisoners

were unfettered. The convict gently rubbed his chafed ankle with a piece of rancid pork fat. Moving his foot to one side, he could feel a small bundle of bones tucked away under his blanket. He had salvaged them from his meat ration and, when the weather was calm and the hatches were removed to admit enough light to work by, he was learning to make 'scrimshaw' – knick-knacks such as toothpicks, dice and rings, carved from bone with the sharpened edge of a spoon. Knives were issued with each meal and collected after it. His neighbour below was busy dismembering a Bible to make himself a deck of cards. From the end of the hold he could hear the slop of the urine tubs, in which blankets were regularly immersed to rid them of lice. The last light faded and he shifted stiffly before seeking oblivion in sleep.

FORCED LABOUR **Under the watchful eye of their overseer, a group of convicts break stones for building the road over the Blue Mountains.**

with them to Australia. In 1789, for example, shortly after the founding of the British colony, the new-comers began to find on beaches and rocks along the shoreline the bodies of dead Aborigines killed by a mysterious malady. The epidemic, which was probably chickenpox, spread along the coasts and far inland, devastating the native peoples. Although a minor 'childhood' infection for Europeans, it was lethal to a population with no previous exposure to it. Similar havoc was wrought by other diseases, including three successive smallpox epidemics.

SAILING WITH THE FIRST FLEET

The British had founded New South Wales, partly to relieve the pressure on overcrowded jails in the home country, and partly to establish a strategic presence in the south-western Pacific. Dutch navigators, notably Abel Tasman, had been among the first Europeans to explore Australia's shores in the 17th century; in 1770, Captain James Cook had landed at Botany Bay and other places on Australia's east coast. Less than 20 years later, in May 1787, the 'First Fleet', with some 570 male convicts, 160 female ones and more than 250 'free' people, had set sail from England, arriving in Botany Bay in January 1788. The commander of the expedition, the naval officer Arthur Phillip, established his headquarters beside a fine natural harbour, later named after the British Home Secretary, Lord Sydney. By 1818, an average of 2500 convicts a year were arriving in New South Wales.

Of the convicts, four out of five were thieves, half of them with previous convictions and a third with four or more. The arriving settler would have recognised most as coming from London, Ireland or from the sooty, slum-circled cities of the industrial north of England. A few were of African and Jewish stock, giving the infant community a varied racial mix. A handful, including some priests and ministers, were political prisoners, guilty of belonging to radical 'corresponding societies', for example, or of anti-British activity in Ireland. Even among the criminal convicts, there were people of education, such as the doctor William Bland, who for various reasons

had strayed beyond the bounds of the law. Almost all were young: some were teenagers, but most were in their mid-20s. Most of the convicts were townspeople by breeding; few made a successful transition to farming. Trade and manufacturing were better propositions, and opportunities were abundant for the energetic. Henry Kable, a Thetford man whose death sentence

THE *LADY SHORE* MUTINY

More than 800 transportation voyages were made between 1788 and 1868, but only one resulted in a successful mutiny – led by guards rather than convicts. In 1797 guards aboard the *Lady Shore* seized the ship in the name of the revolutionary French Republic, claimed political asylum in Montevideo, and sold off the female prisoners as servants to Spanish ladies of quality.

FLOG 'EM AND HANG 'EM After enduring 200 lashes with the cat-o'-nine-tails, this unfortunate convict was then hanged before the strike marks on his back had had time to heal.

had been commuted to life imprisonment, rose to be a convict overseer. After that, he joined forces with another transportee, Henry Underwood, to become a merchant with interests in whaling, boat-building, wholesaling and retailing. James Squire became Australia's first full-time brewer. Simeon Lord became a coal merchant, auctioneer, importer and pioneer manufacturer of woollens, hats and glassware. He eventually became a magistrate, married a fellow ex-convict, had eight children and founded a mercantile dynasty. And no convict left a more lasting legacy than Francis Greenway,

architect of South Head Lighthouse, St James's Church in Sydney, Hyde Park Barracks and the mock-Gothic stables of Government House. Ironically, Greenway was originally transported for forging a building contract.

The population continued to swell as the annual number of transportees peaked at 5000 in the 1830s – a tribute to the efficiency of the British Home Secretary, Sir Robert Peel's newly founded Metropolitan Police in London. Free emigrants also came in increasing numbers, and cattle, sheep and horses multiplied. Some started to run sheep on land beyond the settled area of the New South Wales colony, a practice known as 'squatting'.

At the same time, territorial expansion and injections of capital from Britain created new opportunities for locals. Well-behaved prisoners could be rewarded with a 'ticket-of-leave' which released them from forced labour and entitled them to work for themselves. 'Emancipists' who had worked out their sentence could qualify for 30 acres (12 ha) of land, with another 20 acres (8 ha) for a wife and 10 acres (4 ha) for each child – plus a gang of labourers recruited from those still serving their sentences.

Many convicts, however, persisted in certain kinds of criminality. The standard punishment for drunkenness, thieving, idleness, disobedience and assault was flogging. It was brutal, but swift and cheap. In the 1830s one convict in four was whipped each year, receiving on average over 40 lashes. As late as 1847, a visitor remarked that 'flogging in this

---

DEATH ON THE CHAIN GANG

THE CHAIN GANG was one of the punishments most dreaded by the convicts, as Henry Hale, an old lag, remembered:

❛ For nine months . . . I was on five ounces [140 g] of flour a day; when weighed out, barely four . . . In those days we were yoked to draw timber, 25 in a gang. The sticks were six feet [2 m] long; six men abreast. We held the stick behind us and dragged with our hands. One man . . . was put to the drag; it soon did for him. He began on a Thursday and died on a Saturday, as he was dragging a load down Constitution Hill . . . Men used to carry trees on their shoulders. How they used to die! . . . It was not uncommon for seven or eight to die in one day . . . often while at work. ❜

RELUCTANT WORKERS A woeful group of convicts are assembled for work on the chain gang.

HUSBAND-HUNTING An English cartoon of 1833 satirises the motives of a formidable female emigrant in search of a spouse.

country is such a common thing that nobody thinks anything of it. I have seen young children practising on a tree, as children in England play at horses'.

Female convicts – less than a fifth of all transportees – could not be lashed. Half-rations and fierce purgatives were used when necessary, with persistent offenders put in the chain gang or sent to punishment regimes as at Port Arthur in Tasmania. More fortunate were those who became the common-law wives of officers in the New South Wales Corps. One, the Jewish Esther Abrahams, ended up as the colony's unofficial first lady for six months when her 'husband' George Johnson was the acting governor. They had several children and eventually, after 25 years together, got married.

The treatment of convicts assigned to settlers varied with their masters, but most were at least as well off as they would have been as farm labourers in England. They certainly worked shorter hours – ten from Monday to Friday and six on Saturday. Clothes, mattresses, blankets and cooking utensils had to be supplied by their master, and most were also given a patch of ground to grow vegetables.

Transportation to New South Wales ended in 1840, partly because of political opposition in Britain, and partly because local people began to object to being used as a dumping ground. Tasmania, where the first settlements were founded in 1803, accepted transportees until 1853. Paradoxically, underpopulated Western Australia, founded as a separate colony in 1829, only started to take convicts in 1850 to make good a labour shortage. It continued to welcome them until 1868, when 80 years of transportation involving 162 000 souls were finally brought to an end. South Australia, founded as another colony in 1826, never took convicts.

CREATURES GREAT AND SMALL

Felons were not the only forced migrants. Animals, too, were pioneers. Two bulls and six cows, brought from South Africa by the First Fleet, escaped into the bush and were rediscovered seven years later, now a herd 61 strong. In the hope that the cattle might multiply, it was decreed that the 'mob' – herd – should be left alone. By 1804, it was estimated that there were at least 3000 head of wild cattle.

In 1805, a former officer of the New South Wales Corps, John Macarthur, was granted 5000 acres (2000 ha) of land with a view to developing sheep-rearing and wool production. Under his influence, the tough merino sheep became the colony's dominant breed, although the wool trade's headiest years would come after his death in 1834 on an estate that now covered 60 000 acres (24 000 ha).

Horses, meanwhile, had been introduced from South Africa, with herds of tough, intelligent 'brumbies' multiplying in the wild. Honeybees came in 1822 and found the native eucalyptus much to their liking. The importation of rabbits in 1859 created an infestation that was only eliminated a century later by myxomatosis. Other imported animals included foxes, buffaloes, hares, deer, goats, mice, camels, dogs and cats.

HAPPY ENDING
Mary Haydock, transported as a child, married a ship's officer and then made a fortune.

A SWARM OF SQUATTERS

While some were forced to go to Australia as a punishment, others chose to go –

lured by land and later by gold. These proved powerful incentives in overcoming the

harsh living conditions and the remoteness from civilisation.

SYDNEY IN the early 19th century was a place of colourful bustle. The status of most of its inhabitants was proclaimed by their dress: canary yellow for the convicts, who did most of the menial and laborious jobs; scarlet for the soldiers; plum-coloured swallowtail coats and cream nankeen tights for the merchants; and indigo blue for the 'dungaree men', whose Indian cotton slops (loose overalls) betrayed their position as the poorest of the settler class. The commonest headgear

SETTLEMENT OF SYDNEY Charles Darwin spent an evening walking through the town of Sydney and wrote that he: 'Returned full of admiration for the whole scene. It is a most magnificent testimony to the power of the British nation.'

was a low-crowned, floppy-brimmed hat made from the plaited leaves of the cabbage tree. With the exception of the wealthiest merchants and highest government officials, no one wore socks or stockings and many dispensed with footwear altogether.

On the streets, drunkenness was a common sight, with Bengal rum, a term used for any strong liquor, providing the standard tipple. The Bengal variety, stronger and less sweet than the Jamaican, was sold for 5s a gallon (4.5 litres) and drunk neat by the wineglass. Along the waterfront, whores bargained brazenly with their customers, while drawing on stubby clay pipes stuffed with 'good old Brazil twist'. Hopeful loafers looked for the chance to earn their next drink by carrying a new arrival's

OUTCASTS AND INCOMERS   Aborigines were generally ill-fitted to adapt to urban life. The discarded bottles symbolise the fate that awaited many. Right: An English cartoon pours scorn on the pretensions and easy-going informality of a frontier society.

carpetbag and brass-bound sea chest to a grog house like the 'Black Dog'.

New South Wales' capital was undergoing rapid change, transforming it from a rough-and-ready settlement on the shores of a magnificent harbour into a thriving metropolis. Around the turn of the century, it had boasted scarcely any two-storey houses, and even in the centre most homes had been cottages fronted by gardens. Streets were little more than muddy tracks with pigs rooting for scraps, while the only large buildings were the government offices and military barracks.

Since then, Governor Lachlan Macquarie, a veteran Scottish soldier who presided over the colony from 1810 to 1821, had constructed a central grid of neat thoroughfares, new wharves, two hospitals, a courthouse, well-built barracks to accommodate convicts, and a park. Outside Sydney, he had built roads linking it with inland settlements, including a 100 mile (160 km) road across the Blue Mountains to Bathurst. He had established the Bank of New South Wales and a police force, and had done much to encourage trade, industry and farming in the colony.

By 1827, an anonymous British visitor writing in a local paper was noting, with evident surprise, that 'where I looked for bark huts and weatherboard hovels, I have found streets as long as Oxford Street, and mansions that might do credit to Hanover Square. Such a metamorphosis as . . . Sydney has presented in little more than 30 years, is certainly without parallel in ancient or modern times – the crowded streets – the elegant shops – the London carriages – the stagecoaches, with the guard blowing the horn – the street drays – markets – the women crying fish – the numerous boats and vessels . . . have so bothered me at times, as scarcely to be sensible that I was not in England.'

SQUATTERS' RIGHTS

Unless a poor man arriving as a free settler had a good trade 'in his hands', however, Sydney rarely had much to offer him, and he was forced to sell his labour in a market already swamped with convicts.

BY ORDER OF THE
Colonization Commissioners
FOR HIS MAJESTY'S PROVINCE OF
South Australia
Notice is hereby given,
that from and after the 15th Day of
July next, the Commissioners will
SELL ORDERS
FOR
Town and Country Sections
OF LAND,
Entitling the holders to priority of choice;
and will receive applications from such
intending Settlers as may wish to have
Servants or Labourers conveyed to the
Colony Free of Cost by means of the
Emigration Fund.

The GOVERNOR, COLONIAL COMMISSIONER, and other CHIEF
OFFICERS, will depart about the beginning of the month of SEPTEMBER
next, or as soon as the preliminary arrangements shall be completed.
Copies of the Regulations for the Disposal of Public Land and the Emigration
of Labourers, may be obtained at the Office, No. 61, Lincoln's Inn Fields, where
persons desirous of purchasing Land are requested to apply, & where a Register of
such applications will be immediately opened, & continued in the order of application.
By Order of the Board.
ROWLAND HILL, Sec.

161

LURE OF LAND   The prospect of property attracted
both wealthy and poor emigrants. Left: A land-sale poster aimed at the
rich. Above: A policeman keeps order among prospective buyers, 1876.

Similarly, for the adventurer with a few hundred pounds, it came to be no more than a stopover, where he could get supplies before heading for his ultimate destination – a tract of grazing land, known as a 'run'. The existence of grazing land in the interior had first been discovered by Gregory Blaxland, who in 1813 led the first expedition to cross the Blue Mountains that ringed Sydney. From 1828 onwards, figures such as the army officer Charles Sturt began serious exploration of the Australian interior, followed by Thomas Mitchell, surveyor-general of New South Wales. From the mid 1830s, a boom started in pioneering 'squatters', prepared to carve out a life for themselves in the bush.

By that time, there were three ways for would-be squatters to establish a claim to land in New South Wales, which then encompassed most of the eastern half of the continent. These, in order of frequency, were: buying a 'right of station' from an existing occupant; taking possession of an unoccupied wedge between two occupied areas; and going beyond the farthest settlement into virgin territory. This last method usually involved seeking agreement with one's nearest neighbours on rough boundary markers – rivers, rocks, ridges, or even man-made ditches and plough tracks. Settlers were usually willing to come to an agreement – disputes risked attracting the sometimes unwelcome attention of the authorities and weakened solidarity against later arrivals. However, in the absence of properly surveyed maps, boundaries marked by such ambiguous and vulnerable signs as ant heaps, clumps of scrub, patches of marsh or even notches on tree trunks were always contestable.

Having taken up to a month to choose and mark out a site, the squatter returned to Sydney for tasks such as buying supplies and livestock. Given the crude state of communications outside the area around the capital, the generally low level of vocational skills and the distance between the colony and the mother country, wool was the ideal product for most squatters. It could stand considerable rough handling and suffered little deterioration in transit. Most Sydney capitalists would put up an

SEPARATE ENTITIES

Until the founding of the Commonwealth of Australia in 1901, the Australian colonies were treated independently. The eastern part of Australia, known as New South Wales, was settled from around 1788. Tasmania became a separate colony in 1825. Next was Western Australia in 1829. Then came South Australia in 1836, Victoria in 1851 and Queensland in 1859.

advance equal to twice the squatter's own capital, in return for a third of the profits. To look after a flock of 2000 sheep, a man would also have to hire an overseer, a driver for the bullock-drawn dray which would haul a year's supplies to his land and take his annual clip back to the coast, and four or five more men to serve as shepherds, watchmen and wood-splitters.

Once on site, the men – women were rarely members of the party at this stage – would spend a couple of days building the 'head station', a grandiose name for a couple of flimsy bark hovels. Over the course of time, the wood-splitters would replace them with sturdier huts, made of rough-hewn poles, roofed with thatch or wooden shingles. Even after a decade of occupation, furnishings were likely to remain spartan – beds of sheepskins or possum pelts, a fleece for a door, a tin pan for stewing mutton and a billy-can for tea. Damper – cakes of wheat flour and water, baked in the ashes of a fire – was the staple accompaniment to roasted or stewed mutton.

Smaller 'outstations' were built at strategic points 8 to 10 miles (13 to 16 km) from the head station. As the flock grew, the outstation would be dignified with a shed for storing fleeces and a covered area for shearing. Anything more elaborate, such as a proper barn, a dairy or a ploughed vegetable garden, was out of the question until a definite title to the land had been established. Evident poverty was the best protection from pillaging by bushrangers (escaped convicts living in the bush). At the same time, the more rudimentary the dwelling, the easier it was to dismantle and re-erect, when the stench of sheep dung and decaying carcasses made it desirable to move on.

Each outstation was usually in the hands of two shepherds, who throughout the day drove the flock slowly back and forth across its grazing ground. Hurdles of swamp oak created a stout enough pen to hold 1000 sheep at night. Beside the pen was a sentry box, raised off the ground to keep it clear of snakes and insects, in which the nightwatchman kept an eye open for hostile Aborigines and predators such as wild dogs.

The six weeks of lambing and pitch

branding at the end of June, and the shearing in October, made welcome variations to a dull and monotonous existence. Sheepshearing was preceded by washing – driving the sheep through a river. Shearing was crude, and the fact that each shearer expected four glasses of rum a day did little to add to its precision.

The irksome life of a sheep station made it hard to attract, and even harder to keep, good workers. Those willing to become shepherds could find work so easily that they constantly demanded higher wages and larger rations, and usually refused contracts of longer than three months. Since Aborigines, though good horsemen and good with cattle, were rarely enthusiastic about sheep, labour was sought from as far away as India, China and Chile. The Indians proved tractable but the British government, opposed to the use of 'coloured' labour in the Australian colonies, banned their importation. The Chinese generally absconded; the Chileans rebelled. Fortunately for the squatters, an increase in the immigration of free men in the late 1840s temporarily helped to relieve the labour crisis.

CATTLE, CAPITAL AND COCKIES
The arrival of canning in the 1840s, and refrigeration in the 1860s, opened up a new growth area in farming – raising cattle for beef. This thrived in areas unsuitable for sheep, such

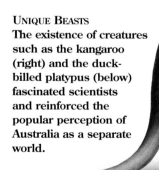

UNIQUE BEASTS
The existence of creatures such as the kangaroo (right) and the duck-billed platypus (below) fascinated scientists and reinforced the popular perception of Australia as a separate world.

ROAD TO MARKET Ox carts transport the wool-clip on the first stage of its journey half-way round the world, from an isolated sheep station on the Murray river to the urban looms of Yorkshire.

as Queensland, carved out of north-eastern New South Wales as a separate colony in 1859. These developments coincided with the first south-north crossing of the continent, by Robert Burke and William Wills and two companions in 1860-1.

Cattle stations demanded a greater investment in buildings than sheep stations – the semiwild beasts had to be penned in fortress-like stockyards of logs, with walls about 6 ft (2 m) high, which could take up to three months to build. As a result, most cattle were left free to graze the unfenced range. Each year neighbours would come together in a general muster, rounding up as many as 20 000 head, sorting out their own branded beasts and sharing out the 'clearskin' – unbranded – calves. Musters were also held on each station to select animals for sale or to stock a new station.

Whether raising sheep or cattle, few squatters were ex-convicts, who tended to prefer town life. Many were men of education; some were local-born sons of officials and merchants. As in other British colonies, there were many from poorer parts of the British Isles, such as Scotland. A substantial group consisted of former officers of the regular British army or East India Company forces, discharged with pensions or put on half-pay as the size of those establishments was reduced. Among them were men such as Kelly of Kamarooka, who brought his pack of hounds from Ireland, and Captain Bunbury, who had left an arm in Navarino Bay (a celebrated naval engagement in 1827 during the Greek War of Independence). Another such figure was Major North, who was over 60 when he started squatting.

A sheep station was cheaper to set up than a cattle one, but even so, with a whole year to wait before the first clip could be sold, a potential owner had to have some capital behind him. It took hundreds of pounds to set up an operation, which drought, disease, fire, flood or a fall in the price of wool could wipe out in a single season.

The sale of the annual wool-clip usually covered running expenses, with long-term profits accruing from the increase in the size of herds. It was a high-risk business, in which fate played as

SHEEP DIPPING Whole herds of sheep had to be dipped at the same time to prevent infections – a task requiring all hands.

THE BIG CLIPPERS Shearing with hand-clippers was still the rule in 1890, when this painting of a gang at work was made. Hard work, a fast pace and a dusty atmosphere built up a big thirst.

much part as judgment in decreeing who made a fortune and who went bankrupt. Few managed to build their fortunes steadily; it was boom or bust – and for many it was bust.

Smaller-scale farmers were slow to establish a presence. However, the growing immigration of free men, not rich enough to be squatters but too ambitious to be shepherds, created a class of would-be yeomen. The occupants of what, by previous standards, were tiny farms were called 'cockatoo farmers' or 'cockies' – possibly because many came from Cockatoo Island, Sydney, a penal settlement founded in 1839.

For all farmers, one of Australia's perennial problems was either too much water or too little. The Hawkesbury River north of Sydney flooded four times between 1801 and 1817, in 1806 washing away the crops of James Ruse – the first freed convict to become a farmer – and bringing New South Wales to the brink of starvation. In 1832, a flood on the Hunter river drowned six people; 20 years later the Murrumbidgee swept away the town of Gundagai altogether, drowning a third of its 250 inhabitants. More often, however, the

BALLADEER OF THE BUSH

ADAM LINDSAY GORDON was born in the Azores in 1833 and educated at the Royal Military Academy, Woolwich, and Oxford. He troubled his wealthy family by spending much of his time with jockeys and boxers. Fearing that his restless spirit would lead him into serious trouble, Gordon's father packed him off to South Australia at the age of 20.

Scorning to use a letter of introduction to the Governor, Gordon – who was a first-class horseman and a powerful swimmer – enlisted in the South Australian Mounted Police as a trooper. He later became a sheep-herder, a horse-breaker, a member of the South Australian House of Assembly and the owner of a livery stable, before winning fame as a champion amateur steeple-chase jockey. He often composed verse while riding, and brilliantly captured the rhythm of a horse at full gallop in *From the Wreck*. He based this ballad on his experience of being sent with a fellow-trooper to warn a signal station of the wreck of the *Admella* near Cape Northumberland:

*And faster and faster across the
  wide heath
We rose till we raced. Then I gave
  her her head,
And she – stretching out with the
  bit in her teeth –
She caught him, outpaced him,
  and passed him, and led.*

Gordon was a loner by nature and educated far beyond those he mixed with, but he also displayed a capacity for 'mateship' and found his best friend in a travelling circus-clown. The bushman's tough but sentimental philosophy found perfect expression in the poet's assertion that:

*Life is mostly froth and bubble,
Two things stand like stone,
Kindness in another's trouble,
Courage, in your own.*

Depressed by money worries, fear of failure as a poet, and constant head-pains following a bad fall, Gordon walked out into the bush and shot himself. He was 47. His collection of *Bush Ballads and Galloping Rhymes* was published on June 24, 1870 – the day of his suicide.

AUSTRALIA'S FIRST FREE FARMER

JAMES RUSE (1760-1837) was born in Launceston, Cornwall, 'bred a husbandman' and convicted on an unknown charge in 1782. Sentenced to seven years' transportation, he spent the first five years on the prison hulk *Dunkirk* at Portsmouth before being sent out with the First Fleet. As Ruse's term expired less than 18 months after his arrival in Australia, Governor Phillip, inspired by the vision of 'emancipists' turned into sturdy yeomen, gave him one cleared acre (0.4 ha) and a patch of raw bush at Parramatta. Captain Watkin Tench, of the Marines, transcribed Ruse's earliest progress: 'I have now an acre-and-a-half [0.6 ha] in bearded wheat, half-an-acre [0.2 ha] in maize and a small kitchen garden . . . My land I prepared thus. Having burnt the fallen timber off the ground, I dug in the ashes, and then hoed it up.' He worked only a small

TAKING A BREAK A lone settler relaxes outside his bark hut. Isolation, hard work and fierce sun made life for settlers very tough.

amount of land each day, 'by which means it was not like the government farm, just scratched over, but properly done. Then I . . . dug in the grass and weeds. This I think almost equal to ploughing . . . And just before I sowed my seed turned it all up afresh. When I shall have reaped my crop, I proposed to hoe it again, and harrow it fine, and then sow it with turnip seed, which will mellow and prepare it for next year.'

As Phillip had hoped, Ruse was able to become self-supporting within a year and survive, with his wife and child, without public charity. His reward was another 30 acres (12 ha) – the first land grant ever made in Australia, aptly named Experiment Farm. By 1819, Ruse had more than 200 acres (81 ha) to his name. However, he ended his days working as an overseer for another farmer, having lost all his own land through failed harvests, rum and labour problems. Nevertheless, the erratically spelled epitaph of Australia's first true pioneer has a special place in its history:

My Mother Reread Me Tenderley
With me She Took Much Paines
And when I arived in This
Coelney
I sowd the Forst Grain and Now
With My Hevenly Father I hope
For Ever to Remain.

---

danger came from drought. When a three-year drought broke in 1829, Governor Ralph Darling of New South Wales ordered a day of thanksgiving. In 1838 a successor, George Gipps, decreed a day of fasting and penitence to break an equally long dry spell. A day of contrition in 1866 brought immediate results on the day it was declared – and another in 1870 was so successful that it was suggested that a day of penitence was needed to make the rains stop.

THE OLDEST INHABITANTS

The tensions with the Aborigines were another potential hazard for settlers in the outback. The first hostilities between whites and Aborigines had

occurred within months of the landing of the First Fleet in 1788. On the frontier of settlement, Aborigines continued to wage war against the intruders on their tribal lands, attacking their livestock and sometimes burning homesteads. Stealth and numbers gave them a few victories but, faced with firearms, their eventual defeat was inevitable.

Only in Tasmania was a deliberate policy of genocide adopted by the colonial authorities, although a month-long campaign in 1830 proved an expensive and futile fiasco. More devastating were efforts to inveigle the Tasmanian Aborigines to settle on Flinders Island in the Bass Strait. Uprooted from their traditional

WELCOME BREAK Bushmen water their horses in the desert.

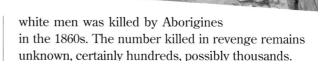

TOGETHER AND APART A 'selector' of the 1880s poses with his family (above). Every willing pair of hands was an asset. Right: Letters from home were the emigrants' essential link to the family and friends they had left behind.

patterns of life, they simply died out, the last survivor dying in 1876.

On the mainland, the Aborigines' decimation was largely a matter of private initiative. Regarded by many settlers as treacherous and subhuman, they were slaughtered – as a precaution, a sport or a vindication of racial superiority. In the view of one colonist in the Port Phillip region (modern Victoria), to regret their disappearance would be 'hardly more reasonable than it would be to complain of the drainage of marshes or the disappearance of wild animals'. Some frontiersmen assisted the process of 'inevitable' extinction by paying for casual labour with flour laced with arsenic.

Attacks on settlers' property and lives were avenged with terrible ferocity. One episode came in 1838 on a property called Myall Creek, towards the border with modern Queensland. In retaliation for an attack on their livestock, a party of white stockmen massacred, more or less at random, a small local tribe of 28 Aborigines, including women and children. When seven of the stockmen were later hanged, it caused outrage among many squatters. In 1857, at Hornet Bank on the Dawson River, a black servant of the Fraser family led some comrades who killed Mrs Fraser, seven of her children and six other people. Retaliatory raids claimed the lives of more than 60 Aborigines. In 1860, the killing of 19 whites at Cullinlaringo produced a reciprocal massacre of more than 170 Aborigines. In north Queensland, it was estimated that one in every ten white men was killed by Aborigines in the 1860s. The number killed in revenge remains unknown, certainly hundreds, possibly thousands.

A GOLDEN AGE

In 1851 the whole of white Australia was bitten by the gold bug or, as the *Bathurst Free Press* put it, 'a complete mental madness'. In that year, gold was discovered first in New South Wales and then in Victoria (which was originally part of New South Wales, and was then settled by Tasmanian sheepmen in 1835 before becoming a separate colony earlier in 1851). The fields in Victoria proved especially rich and the colony's capital Melbourne became virtually a ghost town, as its citizens rushed out to seek their fortunes. In the words of the acting governor Charles La Trobe, writing to the British Colonial Secretary: 'Within the last three weeks the towns of Melbourne and Geelong and their large suburbs have been in appearance almost emptied of many classes of their male inhabitants; the streets which for a week or ten days were crowded by drays loading with the outfit for the workings are now seemingly deserted.'

Life at the diggings was dirty and dangerous. In dry weather, water was so expensive that washing was ignored and shirts were worn till they fell apart. Then when the rain came, it came so abundantly that two or three men a week drowned or suffocated as a result of shafts becoming flooded or collapsing. Mice by the thousand and mosquitoes by the million added to the general discomfort. But

BUSHRANGERS – REBELS AND HEROES

THE WORD 'bushranger' was coined in the first generation of settlement, to describe those for whom the bush was a refuge. Most were escaped convicts who had been lashed beyond endurance, or were fleeing even worse punishment for a crime committed since arriving in Australia. A few were deserting soldiers or sailors.

Also known as 'bolters' or 'banditti', bushrangers lived by armed robbery, murder and arson. They came into their own from the 1820s onwards, when growing prosperity meant that there were more people worth plundering. Their prey ranged from hard-line magistrates to unlucky gold-diggers and innocent, hard-working colonists. Mail coaches were such a routine target that the postal authorities printed a blank form to be filled in by local postmasters, recording that the mails from X to Y had been stolen on such and such a date.

The bushrangers' names – Murphy, Fitzgerald, Donohoe, Kelly – revealed the largest single proportion to have been Irish; most gave their religion as Roman Catholic. They inspired hatred in the authorities, fear in the law-abiding, and admiration among teenage boys and city riffraff. Newspapers were officially hostile, but found that their exploits made irresistible copy. A society created out of former convicts was inevitably bound to uphold the men who defied the police and often made them look absurd, but such notoriety was bought at a high price.

Thanks to the troopers sent to hunt them down with the aid of Aboriginal trackers, bushrangers seldom survived for more than a few years. Most died in shoot-outs or on the gallows. However, their occasional victories became the stuff of legend. Matthew Brady's gang, operating in Tasmania in the mid-1820s, captured and locked up the soldiers sent after them and held the town of Sorell for the night. Another gang in the goldrush days of the 1860s occupied the town of Canowindra in New South Wales for three days. Having rounded up the residents into the hotel, they regaled them with tales of their exploits, 'treated all hands to grog' and offered cigars for which they paid punctiliously.

Ned Kelly, the most celebrated of all bushrangers, was almost the last. Growing up on the borders of Victoria and New South Wales as the eldest of eight fatherless children, he, like his brothers, soon fell foul of the police, who branded the family as troublemakers. When in 1878 Dan Kelly fled after resisting arrest, Mrs Kelly was sent down as an accessory. Swearing revenge, Ned and Dan, with two friends, took to the hills. On October 25, at Stringybark Creek, they intercepted four heavily armed plain-clothes policemen who had been sent after them, and killed three. For the best part of two years, the Kelly gang remained at large, robbing banks and ridiculing the police in a series of statements posted surreptitiously to the Press. Knowing that a shoot-out was inevitable, the young desperadoes prepared themselves by making suits of armour out of ploughshares. Their nemesis came in their home town of Glenrowan, where they shot it out for ten hours with 50 police. Only Ned survived to face the court and hangman, which he did with dignity and coolness. Mrs Kelly sent an admonition from her cell: 'Mind you die like a Kelly, Ned.' And, indeed, his last words on the scaffold were an insouciant, 'Such is life!'

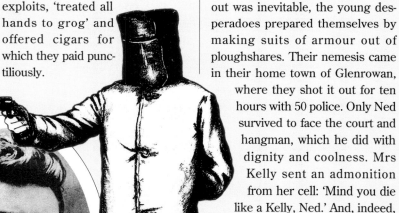

NED KELLY Folk hero Ned's homemade armour saved him in a shoot-out with the police – but he still had to face the noose. After his execution, his shaved head was severed from his corpse.

ABORIGINAL RETALIATION An armed clash between mounted police and Aborigines in 1853. Most confrontations were small-scale, but they cumulatively whittled away the native population.

the lure of gold was irresistible. By the end of 1852, buildings were going up in Melbourne at the rate of 200 a month. In the following year, a prefabricated iron church arrived from Bristol, capable of holding a congregation of 700 and topped by an imposing 40 ft (12 m) tower.

On the whole the diggers were remarkably orderly, although violence did break out in late 1854. Grievances over issues such as a system of licences to obtain the right to dig – charged at a steep 30s (£1.50) a month – and the heavy-handed policing of the gold fields exploded suddenly when a hotel-keeper at Ballarat, north of Melbourne, was acquitted of murdering a miner. In the eyes of the other diggers, this was a monstrous injustice and a group of them set fire to the hotel. After a retrial, the hotel-keeper was found guilty but, at the same time, the leading arsonists were arrested. Calling for a radical overhaul of the colony's administration, some of their fellows resorted to armed resistance. Police backed by soldiers attacked a stockade at Eureka manned by the rebel diggers, with the loss of 34 lives – 30 miners and 4 soldiers. The rebels were

brought to book, but in the longer term many reforms of the kind they had demanded were granted, including the setting up of special courts to arbitrate in gold-field disputes.

Gold left a deep mark on the life of the colonies, symbolised by the term 'digger' which was to become synonymous with 'Australian'. Within eight years of its discovery the population of Victoria, in particular, had increased sevenfold, and the number of farmers grown tenfold to meet the surging local demand for food. In just 15 years, Victoria produced a third of the entire world output of gold. By 1879 Melbourne was laying claim to world-class status as a city, when it hosted an International Exhibition in emulation of similar events in Europe and North America, notably London's Great Exhibition of 1851.

Farming, too, was affected. Squatters and their hands had accounted for a tenth of the Australian colonies' population when

JENNY This picture from the 1840s is an unusually sympathetic portrayal of a Port Sorell Aborigine called Jenny.

BONANZA Australia's gold rushes, like America's, attracted pioneering men from all round the world, reinforcing the restless, go-getting, gutsy character of a society with a new and distinctive character all of its own.

gold was discovered; six years later they were less than one-fortieth. Gold fever infected shepherds, and sheep were left to wander at will. In fact, this proved beneficial. The numbers of sheep grew – no longer cooped up at night they were less prone to footrot. The paraphernalia of stations, hurdles, shepherds and watchmen could be ignored, provided the overall area in which flocks foraged was demarcated and fenced in.

The first fences were of logs or split rails set in posts. By the 1870s, the use of barbed wire had become universal. Enclosed runs ended the old boundary disputes and made 'duffing' – rustling – easier to detect. Encouraged by improved returns, station owners invested in artesian wells, storage tanks and canals, transforming immense tracts of semidesert into good sheep country. In 1851 there were 14 million sheep in Australia; by the 1890s the number surpassed 100 million, and wool accounted for more than half of all exports. Wheat was another boom crop. In 1872, South Australia – a farmer's venture from the start – sent 367 000 bushels of wheat to Britain. In 1873 it sent nearly 3.5 million.

SOMETHING TO CELEBRATE

Public holidays, religion and popular pastimes reflected Australia's

attachment to tradition, combined with a determination to take advantage of

every opportunity for enjoyment.

MELBOURNE ACROSS THE YARRA **The land on which Melbourne was founded was bought from the Aborigines.**

PIONEERING LIFE was dominated by the struggle to survive the elements and subdue the environment. The days set aside for celebration in the Australian colonies represented an effort to bridge the gulf between past and present – the Old World, from which the colonists had been drawn, and the new continent that they were making their own.

The first public holiday was celebrated in New South Wales on June 4, 1788, to mark the fiftieth birthday of King George III. At sunrise, the naval ships HMS *Sirius* and HMS *Supply* fired their cannons in royal salutes. At noon the marines fired three volleys and their band played the national anthem. At 1 pm, and again at sunset, the ships fired further salutes. The Union Jack was flown throughout the day. Governor Phillip and his officers feasted on mutton, pork, fish, fowl and kangaroo, and the convicts were allowed a tot of navy rum to toast the monarch.

Loyalty to the throne thrived throughout the 64 year reign of Queen Victoria. The simple novelty of the postage stamp was one important factor ensuring that her image penetrated even to the remotest corners of the outback. A Presbyterian minister, anxiously venturing into the bush for the first time, was moved almost to tears 'when I reached a lonely hut, and read upon its lintel the two letters VR . . .'

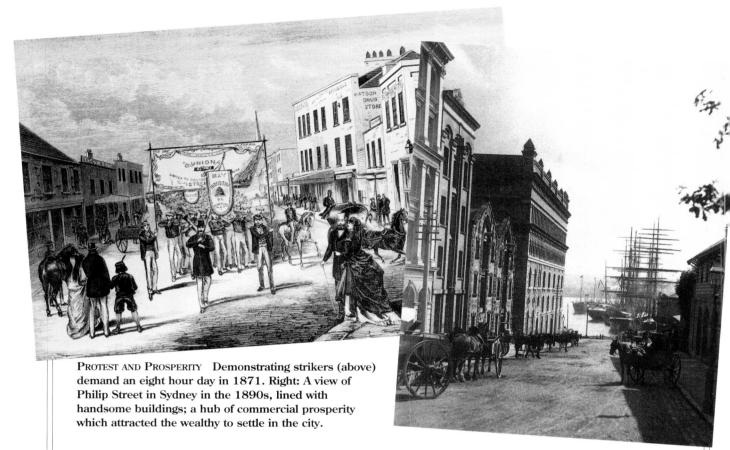

PROTEST AND PROSPERITY Demonstrating strikers (above) demand an eight hour day in 1871. Right: A view of Philip Street in Sydney in the 1890s, lined with handsome buildings; a hub of commercial prosperity which attracted the wealthy to settle in the city.

indicating a letter box, 'I felt that I was still a member of the great British family, and a subject of the British Queen, whom she was caring for even at these ends of the earth. . . .'

The invitation list for the Governor's Ball, held in each colony to mark the sovereign's birthday, became a kind of register of the most eminent and wealthy local citizens. The rest of the populace, meanwhile, made do with military parades, horse-racing, picnics, band concerts and fireworks. On Victoria's birthday, Australians outdid the mother country itself. In Britain the festivities were held on the nearest Saturday; in Australia, regardless of what day of the week it was, people stayed away from work to celebrate.

As early as 1810, governors also recognised St Patrick's Day on March 17 as an opportunity to encourage solidarity among the Queen's subjects, English and Irish, Catholic and Protestant. They met and mingled at a fine banquet and an elegant ball. Outside the governors' residences, the mass of poor Irish, who by mid-century accounted for about a fifth of the colonies' entire population, caroused and rampaged in an unrestrained display

of what was condemned as 'pat-riot-ism'. Drunken behaviour was so commonplace that Protestant newspapers usually bothered to comment only on its absence.

CHURCH AND STATE

Sectarian rivalry affected the evolution of the Australian Sabbath. In New South Wales, Anglicanism was effectively an arm of the state. Convicts who failed to attend worship had their rations cut or were jailed – a policy which soon proved counter-productive. English convicts seldom originated from the Anglican churchgoing classes, and their Irish brethren had little regard for the Protestant liturgy. One victim was Sydney's first church, whose chaplain had personally advanced the money for building it, which was mysteriously destroyed by arson in 1798.

By 1825, however, the colonies were supplied with Nonconformist ministers as well as Anglican and Catholic clergy; Sydney also had a synagogue. For Australians, the Church of England gradually ceased to be *the* Church and had to accept a position of equality with other Christian denominations.

CIVIC PRIDE Melbourne's impressive Public Library was as much an expression of the city's great wealth as it was a tribute to its citizens' thirst for knowledge.

This meant that its clergy were no longer perceived as jailers in clerical disguise. As in Britain, the Church of England tended to attract those who had no other firm commitment.

A common concern of all denominations was that 'there is no Sunday in the bush'. In some settlements, all that distinguished Sunday from any other day was that men put on their weekly clean shirt and the pubs did better business. Paradoxically, and to the great surprise of many visitors, the Sabbath was observed with general decorum on the gold fields. The more perceptive recognised that it was prudent for all to rest on the same day, so that any attempt to infiltrate a neighbour's claim would be instantly detectable. The main beneficiaries were the Methodists. In a situation where there were no places of worship, and where congregations were fluid and alternative distractions few, the Methodists' system of circuit-riding and outdoor preaching was ideal. However, Christmas was one religious occasion with unquestioned appeal

EYEWITNESS

VERANDAHS AND HOSPITALITY

THE ENGLISH NOVELIST Anthony Trollope (1815-82) found much to dislike in Australia. The lack of deference irked him, as did the Australian weakness for 'blowing' – bragging.

But life on a sheep station reminded him of the gracious, spacious days of 18th-century England. Socialising focused on the verandah, which usually ran right round the main house.

❛ Life in the bush would be nothing without a verandah. The men, of course, spend much of their days out of doors, but in the evenings the verandahs are

TRAVEL GUIDE Writing about Australia and its people provided Trollope with much-needed cash.

delightful. Here are congregated lounging chairs, generally very rough, but always comfortable, with tables, sofas and feminine knick-knacks, if there be ladies, till the place has the appearance of a room open to the heavens. The

recreations of the evening consist chiefly of tobacco on the verandah.'

The larger the establishment – some were as big as an English county – the more elaborate the hospitality a visitor might expect: 'A hundred thousand sheep and upwards require a professional man-cook and butler to look after them; forty thousand sheep cannot be shorn without a piano; twenty thousand is the lowest number that renders napkins at dinner imperative. Ten thousand require absolute plenty, plenty in meat, tea in plenty, brandy and water, colonial dishes in plenty, but do not expect champagne.... ❜

THE GREAT OUTDOORS A Victorian picnic is held in the picnic grounds at Hanging Rock. Australia's climate favoured enjoyment of the open air and Australians, who had developed a preference for informality, favoured picnics over dinner parties.

for the bulk of the population. It was observed, as one settler put it, 'in quite John Bull fashion'. A stuffed leg of mutton served as 'colonial goose' and a parrot pie as plum pudding.

By the 1830s, Aborigines had learned to profit from this annual ritual and roamed the streets of Sydney touting fresh-cut greenery as a substitute for holly. In 1852, prospector William Howitt recorded in his diary: 'We shall try to believe it [is] Christmas, [in] spite of the thermometer at 120 [50°C], of diggers' tents in the distance, and the bush around us.' In such circumstances, the Christmas meal might take on the quality of a sacramental penance rather than a secular indulgence.

Francis Hare, another gold-digger, recorded paying an exorbitant price for eggs, suet and raisins, sweating profusely as the resulting Christmas pudding boiled for 24 hours, and then taking a week to digest it.

PROOFS OF PROSPERITY

Falling in the middle of the antipodean summer, Christmas became the nucleus of an extended holiday that stretched from Christmas Eve to the day after New Year's Day. Visitors took it as a proof of colonial prosperity that work could be interrupted for so long in favour of picnics and excursions.

Further proof of the colonies' prosperity lay in a different field. This was the success of building workers in campaigning for an eight-hour day. New South Wales' stonemasons won the right in 1855. Building workers in general won it in Melbourne in 1856, in Queensland in 1858, and in South Australia

SPREADING THE WORD A preacher at the gold-diggings (above) struggles to hold the attention of his congregation. Right: A top-hatted Father O'Donovan inspects the new Catholic church at Gulgong in 1872.

in 1873. By the 1870s, processions of unionists celebrating the anniversary of their triumphs became annual events in Melbourne and Sydney. The novelist Anthony Trollope, writing in the 1870s, though repelled by Australian bragging, readily conceded that for the working man 'these colonies are a paradise', where his table groaned with food and the labour of his hands commanded general respect.

Shorter working hours also meant more time to spare for recreation. Australia's climate favoured outdoor sports, which frequently combined the appeal of manly health-giving exercise with competition, and hence the opportunity to bet on its outcome. Rowing, cricket and 'pedestrianism' – walking – were all immensely popular, but the nearest thing to a truly national sport was horse-racing. The first Australian race meeting was held in Sydney's Hyde Park in 1810. The first Melbourne Cup was run in 1861 in front of 4000 spectators. Within four years,

attendance at the Melbourne Cup had tripled and 'Cup Day' had become an official local half-holiday, with banks and government offices closed for the afternoon. By the 1870s, attendance was up to 30 000 – one in six of Melbourne's entire population – and Royal Navy warships were finding excuses to call in at the neighbouring base of Port Phillip early every November.

The spread of the telegraph enabled punters in the outback to enjoy 'Cup fever' and to organise sweepstakes among their mates. As far away as New Zealand, the race was followed avidly in the Press – even before Australia and New Zealand were joined by telegraph cable in 1876.

New South Wales, meanwhile, had a special holiday of its own. January 26 was Anniversary Day,

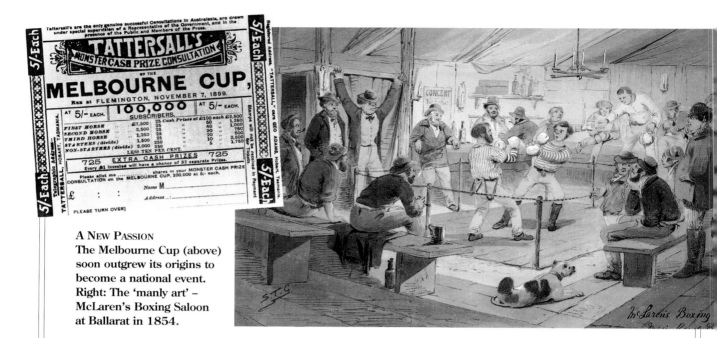

A NEW PASSION
The Melbourne Cup (above) soon outgrew its origins to become a national event. Right: The 'manly art' – McLaren's Boxing Saloon at Ballarat in 1854.

commemorating the first raising of the Union Jack in 1788. Although it had its official aspect, it had become an emancipists' festival in the colony's early days – an occasion for celebration by those who had been transported. Having worked out their sentence and subsequently prospered, the emancipists already regarded themselves as thoroughly Australian and drank to the toast of 'The land, boys, we live in'. As

an affirmation of developing nationhood, Anniversary Day was embryonically a national holiday.

Feasting, excessive drinking and a harbour regatta were the characteristic features of what the *Sydney Gazette* called 'the grand festival of our adopted country'. Unlike Christmas, Anniversary Day provoked no sad memories of home and, unlike the sovereign's birthday or St Patrick's day, it raised no problems of allegiance or belief. It was a holiday, Australian in origin, for Australians – but not for all the country's inhabitants. Other colonies

CRICKETING COUNTRY
An Aborigine plays cricket (above) at Poomindie Mission, South Australia, in 1853. Right: There is standing-room only as an audience watches attentively, despite the absence of seating.

ENGLISH DOWN UNDER

THE AUSTRALIAN scholar E.E. Morris observed in 1898 that 'there never was an instance in history when so many new words were needed . . . for never did settlers come, nor can they ever come again, upon Flora and Fauna so completely different from anything seen by them before'.

Captain Cook recorded 'kangaroo' after his first encounter with Aborigines in 1770. Other words coming from one or other of the numerous Aboriginal languages were adopted for uniquely Australian plants, such as mulga and coolibah trees, and wildlife, such as wombat, wallaby, kookaburra and budgerigar. The newcomers also adopted the Aboriginal word 'jumbuck', to describe an animal they had themselves introduced – the sheep. Another word was 'billabong' – meaning 'river'. 'Boomerang' was one of the few Aboriginal words adopted to describe a man-made object.

The basis of Australian speech was the English of South-east England, and London in particular. The dropped 'h', common among Cockneys, was, however, cancelled out by the strongly emphasised 'h' of the Irish, Scots and East Anglians. As the first generation of Australians were almost all convicts, their speech contained a high proportion of profanity, blasphemy and thieves' slang. In the 1830s, Darwin was shocked to note that, from their ex-convict servants, even the children of officials picked up 'the vilest expressions'. 'Gammon', an 18th-century Cockney word for 'lie', passed into Aboriginal pidgin. 'Swag', originally meaning stolen linen or clothes, came to describe a bundle of personal belongings. A 'swagman' was an itinerant labourer who wandered from one sheep station to the next, with his belongings tied up in a bundle.

New idioms were coined from traditional rhyming slang. An immigrant was a 'Jimmy Grant'. 'Dragging the chain', meaning to work deliberately slowly, clearly originated from the chaingang and came to mean someone drinking too slowly. 'Chunder' – vomit – derives from the long voyage out; an abbreviation of 'watch under' called to warn lower-deck passengers of an imminent threat from above.

Many British regionalisms also survived to gain a wider currency. 'Larrikin', a young tearaway, was once local to the area of Worcestershire and Warwickshire. The 'billy' in which the swagman brewed his tea was originally a 'bally' – a Scottish milk pail. The Suffolk 'cob', to form a friendship, was extended to 'cobber', the friend himself.

As early as 1820, a visitor remarked approvingly of Australian English: 'The children born in these colonies, and now grown up, speak a better language, purer, and more harmonious, than is generally the case in most parts of England. The amalgamation of such various dialects assembled together, seems to improve the mode of articulating the words.' A generation later, however, Australia's school authorities condemned the colonies' common speech as 'coarse, vulgar and representative of all that is least cultivated'. Australians could dissent from that judgment using a rich vocabulary of derision and abuse.

ignored it, and commemorated instead the date on which they were first settled or on which they had gained their autonomy from the supervision of New South Wales.

'Australia,' Trollope noted pointedly in the 1870s, 'is a term that finds no response in the patriotic feeling of any Australian.' Within 30 years, Australians were to prove him wrong after the six colonies finally came together on January 1, 1901, to form the federal Commonwealth of Australia – a self-governing dominion within the British Empire.

ANCIENT AND MODERN
This picture, taken at the turn of the century, shows both Old and New Australians participating (separately) in a public festivity.

INVADING EDEN

The European settlement of isolated New Zealand launched an environmental

revolution which both transformed the local ecology and created a new

economy, heavily dependent on distant markets.

IN MARCH 1828 the *Herald*, a ship carrying missionaries around the coast of New Zealand, pulled into the Bay of Plenty at the northern end of North Island. There they saw a trading ship surrounded by Maoris in canoes, bartering flax, pigs and potatoes for guns and powder.

A few canoes paddled over to the *Herald*, but the Maoris were not interested in the blankets and axes that she had to trade. Continuing along the coast, the scene was repeated. In some places only one canoe came out to greet the missionaries. Even when tempted by canoes laden with pigs and potatoes, the missionaries refused to supply the Maoris with the guns they wanted.

The Maoris' attitude was in sharp contrast to the reception they had given the *Herald* on her first visit to the area four years earlier, when they had happily traded food for fish-hooks and hoes, and

even invited the missionaries to settle among them. What the Maoris now wanted was guns so that they could fight their other Maori neighbours.

The traders who plied the New Zealand shores, many based in Sydney, had originally come to New Zealand in order to supply the whaling ships from Britain, America, France and New South Wales which converged on the plentiful waters of the South Pacific, and which used the Bay of Islands at the northern tip of North Island as a base for refitting and replenishing stores. The whalers in their turn had followed the sealers and timber traders, who in the 1790s were the first Europeans to form temporary settlements there.

In 1814 the first missionaries arrived, drawn by accounts of native people relatively unsullied by contact with Europeans and of their ill-treatment by some ships' captains, who refused to pay for

UNSPOILT NATURE   A view of Lake Wakatipu *c.*1877 by the German painter Eugene Von Guerard.

WHALE NATION The whaling industry played an important part in the early development of New Zealand. Whales yielded meat and also blubber, which was boiled up to release its oil.

supplies or offended against their sacred taboos. This led to reprisals, and in some cases massacre, such as that of the crew of the *Boyd* in 1810. The missionaries were also concerned about supplying Maoris with guns and alcohol.

By 1830 merchants from Sydney and Hobart, principally one 'Johnny' Jones, had decided that permanent shore whaling stations were needed. Together with another merchant, George Weller, Jones made his case in 1839 to a committee of the Legislative Council in Sydney. Jones had already established seven stations in all on the south coast

of South Island, including one at Preservation, three on the Bluff and one at Waikouaiti, and he had purchased thousands of acres of land from the local chiefs. At the time of his submission to the committee, Jones estimated that he had 280 men. In 1840 he sent over agricultural settlers from Australia to Waikouaiti to establish the agriculture on a sound basis.

In 1837 in England, Edward Gibbon Wakefield had formed the New Zealand Association to promote colonisation. Wakefield made planned emigration his lifelong obsession after his experiences in an English prison had convinced him that it was the only solution to Britain's social problems. The association's representatives in New Zealand bought land from the Maoris for resale to settlers. The Maori understanding of land purchase differed from that of the Europeans in that they believed they were agreeing to share their land, not be dispossessed of it. In 1839 the New Zealand Association merged with two other companies to become the New Zealand Company.

Initially, the New Zealand settlements were effectively an offshoot of Australian initiatives, and it was not

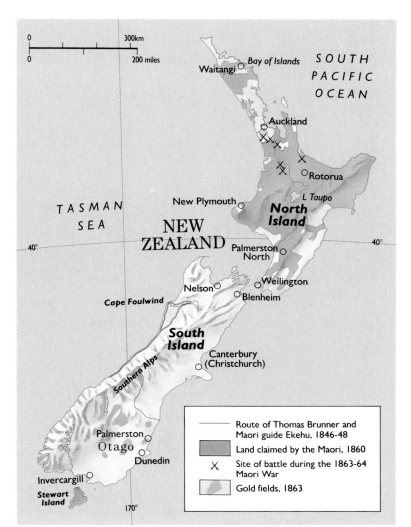

MAORI WARS Expanding European settlements led to conflicts with New Zealand indigenous Maori people.

Map legend:
- Route of Thomas Brunner and Maori guide Ekehu, 1846-48
- Land claimed by the Maori, 1860
- X Site of battle during the 1863-64 Maori War
- Gold fields, 1863

GARDEN OF EDEN

Joseph Banks, the outstanding botanist of his age, landed in New Zealand with Captain Cook in 1769. Of the first 400 plants that Banks examined, he recognised just 14. Later, investigators demonstrated that 89 per cent of New Zealand's native flora were unique to those islands.

until 1838 that the British Government decided upon annexation, which was finally achieved under Governor Hobson in 1840.

After a slow start, the settlement of New Zealand began to gather speed. For those who could afford the passage or could get themselves selected for sponsorship by a charity, the promise of a new life in a new land could seldom have seemed more attractive – even if it was four times as far away as North America. The MP and engineer George Rennie, addressing fellow Scots in 1843, appealed to men hungry for work and land to look farther afield and to look together: '. . . there is land enough and to spare in the colonies. Though any one of you . . . would feel himself among a strange people and strange ways, that need not be the case if a number of us resolve to go together . . . In any climate nearly approaching to our own, a knot of us can make at any time a Scotland for ourselves . . . A party has been formed for the purpose of making a settlement in New Zealand.' Rennie, however, did not go out there. Instead, he took over his father's engineering business.

SEPARATED SETTLEMENTS

On the North Island, major settlements were established at Auckland, Wellington and New Plymouth. Auckland, founded as a seat of government in 1840 by Governor Hobson, was built on a site vacated by local Maoris in return for bundles of clothes, food

TAMING THE WILD   This 1876 view shows an early settlement with a railroad, a bridge, a road and a church.

and tobacco and £30 sterling. The other settlements were the result of private initiative by the New Zealand Company. Wellington, which was set on a windswept slope around a deep, sheltered harbour, also dates from 1840. It was named after Britain's foremost military hero – a personal supporter of the New Zealand Association. New Plymouth was settled by migrants from Devon and Cornwall.

On the South Island, Nelson, named after Britain's greatest naval hero, was settled on New Zealand Company land in 1842. Land was distributed by lottery – in front of a breathless audience, cards bearing the names of settlers were drawn from revolving drums by little boys. But a year later the town site was still covered by a thigh-high blanket of fern. The thick, subtropical bush of the area was so forbidding to newcomers, largely unskilled in agriculture, that men had to be sent out in gangs to slash it down. By 1844-5 many families were reduced to a diet of potatoes. However, salvation

COURTING DANGER
Descending a 100 ft (30 m) sheer cliff on a makeshift ladder actually appealed to some adventurous spirits.

came in the 1850s when sheep-raising for wool, which was relatively easy to export, proved more profitable than growing crops. In the 1860s Nelson grew rapidly, thanks to the gold rush.

Dunedin, also on the South Island, was luckier. Founded in 1848 by Scottish Presbyterians, it was to prosper so much from the discovery of gold nearby in 1861 that, for a while, it became the

---

MARITIME GASTRONOMY DEFEATS A FRENCHMAN

IN 1842, the Catholic missionary Father Jean Forest endured a nine-day voyage by coastal cutter from Auckland to the Bay of Islands. The catering arrangements proved less than satisfactory:

❛ Some water was boiled and I do not know if it was tea that was added, but they took an old tin cup (used also for feeding the dogs and a little pig), wiped it carefully with a very dirty pocket handkerchief, doubtless to show me how clean they were, then they added brown sugar, stirred the potion with a long knife, tasting it at the same time. Finally they poured me out a generous helping . . . With this I was given a biscuit smeared with discoloured fat from the plate on

which yesterday's pork had been placed . . . You can imagine how quickly my breakfast was over!

Cook had prepared dinner. He had boiled in seawater some pork so dirty as to be unrecognisable. Afterwards some potatoes were boiled in the same water . . . The meal was served in an old tin dish . . . They did not use the handkerchief to clean this, but the cook rubbed it on his vest and trouser . . . They had only one old knife . . . For forks they imitated the Maori and used their fingers. Each in turn took the piece of meat and the knife in his hands and cut off pieces which, without exaggeration, weighed at least a pound . . . My turn came. Naturally I was much

embarrassed . . . and looked round for a piece of stick I could use for a fork, but this provoked derisive laughter at my refinement . . . On Monday morning . . . provisions were exhausted . . . The captain announced that he had no money . . . and took a little collection . . . [In the evening, once landed, he] went . . . to the wretched hut of a poor European where he purchased a few pounds of pork which the dogs had killed in the forest . . . It was still covered with blood and mud. Traces of the dogs' teeth were still visible and the hair was still on the skin . . . They put it just as it was into the old pot . . . I managed to live for the rest of the time on potatoes and biscuits. ❜

leading settlement in New Zealand. Its university, the University of Otago, founded in 1869, was the first in the whole of New Zealand and Australia.

The socially conservative, homeward-looking tone of embryonic New Zealand society was reflected in many of its place names. A Scottish strain was particularly marked, especially in the South Island where there were settlements named Balmoral, St Andrews, Roxburgh, Invercargill, Clyde, Glenary and Heriot. Natural features were also given Scottish names. There was even another Ben Nevis.

Living conditions in the earliest days were often primitive, especially in the remoter parts of the South Island. James Adam, who later became a prominent citizen of Dunedin and the surrounding Otago district, relates how he carved and wove – as much as built – his first dwelling: 'There was a clump of maple trees, but before cutting them down, I stretched a line through them for the ground plan of the house; trees which coincided with this line I left standing, merely cutting off the tops, and those which were out of the line were cut down and put in the line by digging holes . . . The natives [Maoris] then put small wands or wattles

ADVERT **This picture was used to sell 'Tents for travellers and emigrants'.**

across the uprights about twelve inches [30 cm] apart, fastening them firmly with strips of flax, and over all they laced the long grass to the wattles, did the same over the roof, and at the end of four days my house was habitable.' By contrast, dwellings in Canterbury, the district around Christchurch, were built of sawn lumber – some based on frames brought from England. Even in Auckland, which had by far the largest concentration of European settlers, social life was still sparse in the 1850s. According to William Swainson, Attorney-General for New Zealand for 15 years: 'Once a week during the summer months the regimental band plays for a couple of hours on the well-kept lawn in the Government grounds . . . two or three balls in the course of the year; as many concerts; an occasional riding party, picnic or water-party; fern-hunting . . . Now and then a ship of war enters the port; and occasionally Auckland is visited by some company of travelling players. . . .'

According to Swainson, the local youth had to content itself with 'dissipation in the milder form of temperance and tea meetings' or watching the occasional cricket match between teams picked from the military and civilian communities. Winter mud hampered socialising, especially in the evenings, as there was no street lighting and many streets 'existed but on paper'. Undeterred, would-be dancers often struggled through the slosh to the house of their hostess, the men carried on the backs of obliging Maoris, the ladies having to make their own way, holding up their dresses and wearing jackboots borrowed from

LAND OF HOPE **Emigrants land at Jackson's Bay on New Zealand's South Island, having travelled there on SS *Grafton*.**

JACKS OF ALL TRADES

THE PIONEER life placed a premium on versatility. Men had to be infinitely adaptable if they were to succeed. Few were exempt from the restless urge to try for improved prospects in a better place. Charles Money, a penniless middle-class bachelor, had no less than 14 different 'skills' and 41 changes of job in seven years. Nine times he tried his luck as a prospector, six times he worked in constructions, and seven times he trudged through the bush as a backpacker of goods. Three times he held commissions in the Colonial Defence Force, and he even ran a circulating library – before returning to England. But he was by no means unique.

THE OPEN ROAD
Pioneers travelled the country in search of work.

Henry Scott, during his first three years in New Zealand, worked as a labourer on a farm and a sheep station, supervised a shearing shed, prospected for gold, ran a horse team, shot wild pigs, cleared tracks through the bush, collected newspaper subscriptions, and served as a policeman before eventually settling down as a journalist.

Such wanderlust may have been extreme, but many small farmers in need of cash had to 'moonlight' by doing a variety of jobs such as navvying, felling trees, shearing, harvesting and fencing, or by working as part-time dealers in livestock, lumber or produce.

Another example was Richmond Hursthorse, who was born in New Plymouth in 1845,

and moved with his parents to Nelson in 1860. Two years later, he was serving with the bushrangers. Between 1868 and 1875, he prospected in three gold rushes and worked in Melbourne as an engineer. He settled in Nelson as a farmer and entered politics, before moving on twice more and finally dying back in his birthplace.

George Pain worked on a farm and a sheep station until he had saved £100 from horse-dealing on the side. He used the money to buy a stock of clothes and become a travelling salesman – and in just three months he had lost everything to the lure of gold. He took to the road again and within three years he had saved enough to buy a 100 acre (40 ha) property. At the time of his death, he was the owner of a general store, several large sheep stations and a brick works.

their menfolk, as it was considered improper for a woman to be touched by a Maori.

The early settlements were not only isolated from the outside world but were also isolated from each other. Travel inland was difficult due to the rough terrain, the density of the forests, dangerous rivers and areas of swamp, although there were those who undertook trips of exploration in search of new grazing land. One such was a young surveyor, Thomas Brunner, in the employment of the New Zealand Company, who in 1846 travelled down the west coast of South Island in search of tablelands that he had heard about from the Maoris. 'Rain continuing', he wrote. 'Food scarce,

GAMING HOUSE In the late 1890s Grahamstown was a small frontier town – but it could still boast a casino.

strength decreasing, spirits failing, prospects fearful.' However, he struggled on, reaching Tititira Head where he decided to stop, as he had broken his leg. On his return journey, Brunner reached Nelson again in June 1848. He had taken 550 days to cover approximately 300 miles.

HOME COMFORTS Above: A hard-working family pose proudly before their house and well-tended garden. Left: The settlers were highly skilled in making do. Lacking furniture for storage, early settlers used hooks and shelves instead.

In 1860 an overland communication between Auckland and Wellington – a distance of 437 miles (703 km) – was established. Maori couriers made the trek on foot every fortnight, taking 25 days or more to complete the journey. Official correspondence between the two places could take up to five months there and back. It was often faster to correspond via Sydney, 1200 miles (1900 km) away.

A PARADISE FOR PRACTICAL MEN

The English novelist Samuel Butler (1835-1902) who, having quarrelled with his clergyman father, went to New Zealand to become a sheep farmer, noted how colonists tended to view their surroundings in purely practical terms: 'A mountain here is only beautiful if it has good grass on it. Scenery is not scenery – it is "country" – if it is good for sheep, it is beautiful, magnificent and all the rest of it; if not, it is not worth looking at.'

Few settlers were prepared for the dramatic elemental shocks in New Zealand – flash floods, landslides, gales and unpredictable frosts. In the North Island, they found volcanic mountain chains where most of the volcanoes were still active – with an abundance of hot springs and geysers to prove the continuing activity. Earthquakes, too, were frequent. Wellington, for example, has on average one minor earthquake every year; one severe tremor in 1848 damaged all but four of its 46 brick houses, demonstrating that the building techniques of the home country could not always be translated straight to the new settlements. The South Island,

A DAY IN THE LIFE OF

A SHEEP-STATION CHILD

TEN-YEAR-OLD Mary Kelley wriggled her bare toes with boredom and stared out at the rain. It had rained all morning, it had rained all day yesterday, and for all she knew it would rain for the rest of the week. There was no one to talk to and nothing to do. But that wasn't too unusual – there were very few distractions in the isolated spot where they lived. Her father and brothers were mending fences at the far end of the run and had taken all the dogs with them. Her mother had gone to stay with Mrs MacDonald, their nearest neighbour, two miles away along the valley. She wouldn't be back until Mrs Mac's baby was born.

ISOLATION **Although many of the rural areas looked idyllic, loneliness was often a problem and lively minds were often bored.**

Without the boys to tease and annoy her, Mary had finished almost all of her chores quickly: Ben's torn shirt was mended; the washing hung steaming near the iron stove; the bare wooden floor was swept; and she had even swept the verandah, just for something to do.

She glanced up at the faded portrait of Queen Victoria on the wall and wondered what London was like. Then she looked down, only to see the word 'London' on the manufacturer's label of her mother's new sewing machine – something she was strictly forbidden to touch. Sighing, she pulled a stool up to the scrubbed wooden table and, as the sky darkened, began to peel potatoes for the evening meal. She glanced again at the window. Still no sign of anyone. Another little sigh escaped her, as she wondered whether tomorrow would be any different.

meanwhile, presented the immigrants with Alps worthy of Switzerland and fiords and glaciers worthy of Norway.

Added to this, the early newcomers found themselves in a land where there were almost no useful sources of food, either plants or animals. However, plants and animals introduced from other parts of the world flourished with extraordinary abundance. Within less than a decade of its foundation, Christchurch had a livestock population which included 6000 horses, 35 000 cattle and almost a million sheep; the town was also soon obliged to spend £600 a year just to clear its River Avon of clogging watercress. The animals, too, suffered sharp shocks. Lady Barker, patron of an Otago station, lost half her cattle and nine-tenths of her sheep in the terrible snowstorms of 1867. And the routine of tending livestock could prove laborious, as Samuel Butler soon discovered. 'Long wearisome rides and walks in search of truant cattle and sheep, bivouacs night after night on the damp, cold ground, mutton, damper [bread] and tea (and that colonial tea!) at breakfast, dinner and supper . . . with a choice of passing the night on some bleak mountain top or wading through an unexplored swamp . . .' But, arduous though it was, such labour was profitable – Butler doubled his capital in less than five years.

PROUD MOMENT **A giant cabbage is recorded for posterity, before being consigned to the cooking pot.**

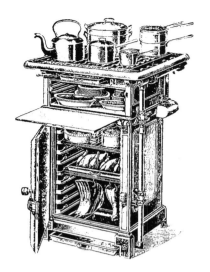

By the 1890s there were three cattle and five sheep for every two humans in New Zealand.

Unlike Australia, New Zealand society was essentially the product of voluntary rather than forced migration, and the New Zealand Company declined to take young male 'pardoned' petty criminals. Generally speaking, the higher up the social scale newcomers were, the less they were prepared to adapt to local conditions. On formal occasions, at least, the would-be elite clung to their starched collars and multilayered petticoats, looking down on the corduroy, jersey and tartan of their neighbours and the bare feet of their neighbours' children.

But even the better-off could be reduced to hardship by the unexpected. When fire swept through the newly built *raupo* (bullrush) home of surveyor Edwin Harris, he lost not only all his surveying instruments but virtually everything his family owned. So few of their neighbours had anything to spare that Mrs Harris was forced to rummage through the ashes to scavenge what she could of

HOME ON THE RANGE **Adverts for domestic appliances showed an idealised view of food availability.**

her incinerated household, making shoes out of the scorched cloth for her three children. It was 12 months before another complete outfit of clothing arrived from England.

The 1874 census showed that there were more than 40 000 single men over the age of 20, but only 7000 single women. In a book about New Plymouth, Charles Hursthouse, an enthusiastic promoter of emigration who made a succession of visits to New Zealand, warned intending settlers that if they had an extra week to spare before departure, they would be wise to spend it looking for a wife rather than for a thoroughbred horse or the latest plough. Single men who worked hard and did well by colonial standards were often embittered to find that they had done little to enhance their marriage prospects. As Robert Petch, the occupant of a 'first-rate rough strong hut', wrote in 1880: 'For an English girl accustomed to society and flying

TOWN PLANNING **From the 1850s, builders used mass-production methods, enabling them to provide more houses.**

PIONEER SOCIETY   As can be seen in this social occasion, settlers tried to live as if they were still in the Old Country.

round to parties, towns, etc, to come and settle as a squatter's wife out here I think is rather out of the question.'

Alcohol became a refuge for many such men. Drunkenness had been the country's most prevalent social evil from the start, accounting for more than half of all criminal convictions. The clear association between habitual intoxication, disorderly conduct, petty theft and domestic violence provoked the emergence in the 1880s of a temperance movement which was well-supported, particularly by women. The movement created a tide of female influence which led to them demanding – and being granted – the vote in 1893, making New Zealand women the first in the world to win the right to vote in national elections.

ANOTHER ALBION

The emigrants who came to New Zealand fell into three broad categories. Most numerous, though accounting for less than 50 per cent by the 1880s, were those who came direct from the British Isles. They were largely from the lower-middle and working classes and, in contrast to most migrants to Australia who came from the cities, they came mainly from villages and small towns, particularly in the south of England and Scotland. The second group came from other settler societies, such as Australia, South Africa and the US, especially during the New Zealand gold rush of the 1860s. A third group consisted of cultural minorities, mostly from Germany and Scandinavia, and to a much smaller extent, from southern Europe and Asia.

By the 1880s a significant proportion of New Zealand's non-Maori population was native-born. Even so, the assumption of Anglo-Saxon cultural superiority, a belief in the essential rightness of European institutions, the predominance of Protestant Christianity, and a warm attachment to the 'home country' and its sovereign, were accepted readily by almost all, whether directly British or not. Mormons, Quakers and Chinese emigrants, however, did not find themselves particularly welcome.

The 'Britishness' of emigrant settlements in New Zealand was often striking to newcomers. As the visiting American novelist and travel writer Mark Twain put it in the 1890s: 'It was Junior England all the way to Christchurch – in fact, just a garden. And Christchurch is an English town, with an English park . . . and a winding English brook just like the Avon – and named the Avon . . . It is a settled old community, with all the serenities, the graces, the conveniences, and the comforts of the ideal home life. If it had an Established Church and social inequality it would be England all over again with hardly a lack.'

ALIEN AESTHETIC **Early artists were fascinated by the unfamiliar skills of the Maori carver or tattooist, and took careful pains to record both the decoration of houses (above) and faces (left).**

Social inequality was, indeed, much less marked than in Britain, and New Zealand was far in advance of the home country in nurturing the rights of all its people. It was to be one of the first countries in the world to establish secular education (in the 1860s), enforce industrial arbitration (in 1894), and set up old-age pensions (in 1898).

The New Zealand way of life reflected nostalgia for Britain, with only a few adaptations to match local circumstances. To catch the best of the sun, houses were built with their verandahs facing north rather than south. Some homes were smaller than they would have been 'back home', reflecting the high cost of skilled labour and building materials. Furnishings were often simple. Nevertheless, there were few rows of pinched terraced houses, and almost every dwelling, however humble, was surrounded by its own garden, usually with a vegetable patch and often an orchard.

The diet, meanwhile, combined a traditional relish for beef and tea with a willingness to experiment with mussels and snapper, pigeon stew and even, outside the towns, to tackle fern root and kumara – the sweet potato which for centuries had been the staple food of the Maoris. As sources of food and for the purposes of sport, dozens of species of wildlife were imported from overseas by New Zealand's 'acclimatisation societies', bringing in not only game birds and fish, but also deer, chamois, moose, wallaby and possum. During the 1850s, rabbits were introduced, rather disastrously. By 1876, one station in Otago was employing 16 men and 120 dogs simply to keep down the rabbits, killing 36 000 a year. On the other hand, the skins could be sold for twopence each, and by 1881 represented the country's seventh largest export.

WALL OF FOOD

In 1844 the chiefs of Waikato staged a feast at which Robert Fitzroy, governor of New Zealand, was the guest of honour. The central feature of the banquet was a rampart of potatoes 7 ft (2 m) wide, 4 ft (1 m) high and 400 yd (365 m) long, surmounted by a fence draped with thousands of dried dogfish.

UNIVERSAL CURRENCY In this mid-19th century drawing, a sailor barters his tobacco in exchange for Maori potatoes and pumpkins.

Shooting and wood-chopping competitions celebrated essential rural skills. Rivers, stocked with salmon and trout from 'home', delighted anglers, and highland hotels replicated their Scottish originals, complete with libraries of fishing books, malt whisky and roaring log fires. Each settlement made the anniversary of its foundation a special day – more often two – for celebration. At Auckland, which looked to the sea for its fortune, the central focus of the junketing was a regatta; at agricultural Nelson, it was a ploughing match.

Cultural life was vigorous rather than distinguished. There were local newspapers but at first few locally published books or magazines, although these became more common as the population expanded to a size that made them profitable. Nor was there much taste for a literature that reflected the realities of frontier life. In the 1850s Sarah Selwyn, an early colonist, declared: 'We had enough of the real thing, and wished for a different atmosphere from travels in the bush and settling, sheep runs and squatting. . . .' Choral singing from cheap Novello editions was very popular, growing naturally out of church

attendance. Pipe bands were encouraged by the significant number of pioneers of Highland origin in settlements like Dunedin. Education was regarded as important, but mostly in a practical sense. As settler Arthur Clayden reported in 1884: 'The universal test of merit is success; the ideal colonist is one who yesterday had not the proverbial halfcrown in his pocket, and today can write his name to a £50 000 cheque.'

AN ECOLOGICAL REVOLUTION

When the Maoris arrived in New Zealand from Polynesia in about AD 800, they entered a land that had been isolated from the rest of the world for 50 million years. They found worms as long as a man's forearm, and moas – flightless birds that stood almost twice as high as a fully grown adult. The only indigenous mammal they encountered was the bat. They brought with them the dog, more as a delicacy than as a companion, and – unintentionally as a stowaway – the rat. Living simply as hunters, gatherers and gardeners, the Maoris made an impact on the local ecology that was significant, if gradual. Their fires, deliberate or accidental, began the long process of converting drier forests to open country. By the time of Captain James Cook's first landing in 1769 on the north end of the South Island, their hunting prowess had rendered the moa extinct.

SHOWING THE FLAG Coastal shipping was an important adjunct to New Zealand's undeveloped road system.

DWARFED BY NATURE The natural beauty of the forests remained largely unscarred until the arrival of steam-powered machinery, which enabled settlers to chop down and use many more trees for building.

Although for half a century, few white intruders went far enough inland to leave the sound of the surf behind them, their arrival rapidly began to change the local ecology. Cook planted some potatoes in 1773 and found the vegetable still growing when he returned two years later. The Maoris were experienced cultivators of tubers such as the kumara sweet potato, and they welcomed the common potato, delighted to find that, unlike their existing root crops, it flourished as well in the cooler South Island as in the North. It also had the advantages of maturing quickly and requiring little attention between planting and harvesting. Unlike the kumara, it could be stored with little regard for temperature or humidity. With the potato, the Maoris were able not only to extend cultivation and sustain more of their people, but also to produce a food surplus to exchange with ship-borne whites for the products of their technology. Potatoes may also have given them more time for their favourite occupation – warfare.

In 1769 the French explorer Jean de Surville gave a pair of hogs as a present to a Maori chief, urging him to breed from them; and shortly afterwards, in 1773, Cook deliberately liberated pigs, goats, geese and poultry to breed at will in the South Island. The abundant shade, moisture and succulent fern roots made New Zealand a paradise for pigs. Wild ones – still called 'Cookers' – soon roamed in great herds, the largest boars attaining twice the weight of a man. Like the potato, pigs provided the Maoris with an additional food source as well as a trading asset.

A LETHAL IMPACT

These European 'gifts' enriched both native and visitor alike, but Europe's diseases did not. Centuries of isolation and a consequent lack of familiarity with most mammals – hosting infection-carrying parasites – combined to render the Maori highly vulnerable to new threats. Aspects of their culture simply made these even more deadly. Among the Maoris, the sick were routinely immersed in cold water to purify them – a procedure virtually guaranteed to induce pneumonia. Blankets were worn until they were matted with filth, even when soaked with rain, leading to chills and fevers. Sexual relations with Europeans exposed the Maoris to venereal infection and tuberculosis – 'occupational diseases' for the passing European or American seaman.

NATURAL SYMBOLS The distinctiveness of New Zealand's flora and fauna readily supplied it with national symbols such as the kiwi (left) and the fern.

UNDER FIRE
Settlers often
found themselves
facing Maori
raiders. Below:
Relations
between Maori
and settler
deteriorated soon
after the signing
of the Treaty of
Waitangi.

A PUBLIC MEETING

Will be held at the Exchange, Te Aro, on Wednesday evening, April 20, at 7 o'clock precisely, to consider the late aggressions of the Natives at Porirua, Wanganui, and elsewhere, and the best steps to be taken with regard to the lands chosen by the Colonists and of which they are unable to obtain possession in consequence of the alleged claims of the Natives.

An early attendance is particularly requested. It is hoped the Company's Principal Agent, the Chief Police Magistrate, and the Protector of Aborigines will attend on this important occasion.

Manners-street, April 16, 1842.

Printed at the "Gazette" Office, Port Nicholson.

The biological invasion of New Zealand intensified in the two decades after the permanent white settlement began in the North Island in 1814. Here, newcomers obtained 200 acres (80 ha) of land in return for 12 axes. With them they brought wheat, vegetables, fruit trees, horses, cattle and sheep.

It took them more than a decade to make their first Maori convert to Christianity. As the blacksmith at one mission sourly observed in 1824: 'Their objective in letting us live amongst them, is to get all they can from us.'

Conversion to European-style agriculture proved a much speedier process, as the Maoris enthusiastically raised maize, onions, cabbages, pork and potatoes to trade with passing whalers. Later they would export the same produce to Australia, over 1000 miles (1600 km) away, sailing their own Western-style ships. But, unlike the native peoples of North America, the Maoris were not tempted by blankets, mirrors, glass

EYEWITNESS

GOD PREPARES THE WAY

IN 1837 New Zealand's official British Resident, James Busby, reported to the Colonial Secretary in London on the conditions of the Maori people:

❝ Disease and death prevail even amongst those natives who, by their adherence to the missionaries, have received only benefits from English connections; and even the very children who are reared under the care of missionaries are swept off in a ratio which promises, at no very distant period, to leave the country destitute of a single aboriginal inhabitant. The natives are perfectly sensible of this decrease; and when they contrast their own condition with that of the English families, amongst whom the marriages have been prolific in a very extraordinary degree of a most healthy progeny, they conclude that the God of the English is removing the aboriginal inhabitants to make room for them. ❞

beads or alcohol. What they craved was muskets. Much of the time the Maoris hunted each other. They fought to revenge an insult, a trespass or a killing. They fought for land or control of a favoured anchorage. They also fought for reputation and the *mana* (prestige) that came with the fruits of victory. To this day the remains of some 6000 fortresses confirm that warfare was endemic among them. In 1814, a single gun could command a price of eight hogs and 150 baskets of potatoes. With muskets, a chief and his tribe could enslave their neighbours; without them, they themselves would be enslaved.

In 1820 Hongi Hika, chief of the Ngapuhi tribe in the North Island, went to England where he was presented with numerous gifts. In Sydney, on his way back, he exchanged the gifts for muskets. Emboldened by his technological advantage, Hongi Hika launched a series of genocidal wars which soon claimed thousands of lives, including his own. In the years 1830 and 1831 alone, Sydney exported to New Zealand more than 8000 muskets and 70 000 lb (32 000 kg) of powder. The wars of these decades cost anything from 20 000 to 80 000 Maori lives and forced 30 000 people to flee their ancestral lands.

Meanwhile, the biological invasion broadened and deepened. When Charles Darwin visited the area around the Bay of Islands in 1832, during the voyage of the *Beagle*, he noted the presence of the common dock, which 'will, I fear, forever remain a proof of the rascality of an Englishman who sold the weeds for those of a tobacco plant'. Turnips, radishes, garlic, celery, cress and even peach trees all escaped domesticity to grow luxuriantly in the wild. White clover, by contrast, got off to a shaky start. Deliberately sown by the missionaries

STATUS SYMBOL
A formal painting of a Maori depicts him with his prize possession – a gun.

MEN OF GOD   **Native New Zealanders arrive by boat to worship at the Wesleyan mission station at Waingaroa.**

as fodder for cattle, it flourished at first, but failed to reseed itself and had to be replanted every season. The missing element, an effective insect pollinator, was supplied in 1839 by Miss Brumby, sister of a missionary, who introduced the honeybee at Opononi, North Island. Two hives brought from England were thoughtfully placed in the mission graveyard – 'this place being considered the most free from possible disturbance through the curiosity of the Natives'. Fortified by reinforcements in 1840 and 1842, the insects prospered, swarming and pollinating clover plants by the million and providing their keepers with abundant supplies of honey and wax as valuable by-products.

PIONEERS IN THEIR OWN LAND

For many Maoris, the devastation wrought by European disease far outweighed the benefits of new crops and livestock. As one missionary reported: 'They charge us as the authors of their evils . . . Till we came among them, they say, young people did not die but all lived to be so old as to be obliged to creep on their hands and knees. Our God, they say, is cruel; therefore, they do not want to know Him.' Rejection was one reaction; reinterpretation was another. One cult combining

BEARING WITNESS
Left: The christening taking place in this Gothic-style church shows just how literally the settlers maintained Old World customs and styles. Below: The title page of a Maori edition of the Bible.

Maori and Old Testament ideas began to gain currency during the early 1860s. Its followers believed that strict obedience to their leader Te Ua, a local prophet from the Taranaki region on the southwest of North Island, and to his creed would make them invulnerable in battle to bullets, if they raised their right hands and cried *'Pai marire, hau! hau!'* ('Good and peaceful, Amen, Amen'). Unfortunately, this notion helped to prolong inter-tribal wars in the Taranaki area.

Despite their misgivings, many Maoris were making a sustained effort by the 1830s to learn the ways of the settlers. In the 1830s Darwin was impressed by what he saw of this at a mission station at North Waimate on the Bay of Islands: 'The lesson of the missionary is the enchanter's wand. The house had been built, the windows formed, the fields ploughed and even the trees grafted by the [native] New Zealander. At the mill, a New Zealander was seen powdered white with flour, like his brother miller in England.' The Maori children had even learned to play cricket.

In 1837 a petition was sent by 200 missionaries and settlers to the British Government, asking it to extend its protection over them. London was eager to forestall a possible takeover of New Zealand by the French, but dreaded adding yet another territory to the costs of the Empire. But the prospect of an outlet for British emigrants which could be self-sustaining, rather than a drain on the homeland, tipped the balance. Colonisation societies worked hard in support of this vision. An existing landholder – of 150 sq miles (390 sq km) – assured the hesitant that 'a person must be uncommonly hard pushed if he cannot get a living in New Zealand, it being the best poor man's country in the world'.

FIGHTING SPIRIT

In 1863, at the height of the inter-Maori wars, a British force surrounded an improvised fortress at Orakau and bombarded its 300 defenders ceaselessly for three days. When called on to surrender, the Maori commander defiantly replied: 'Friend, I shall fight against you for ever, for ever!' As the British launched their final assault, the Maoris made an orderly retreat and escaped – to fight on.

In 1840 Maori chiefs met at Waitangi, with representatives of the British Government, to discuss a British offer of annexation to the Crown in return for the Maoris being assured full possession of their lands. A Maori tribal chief, Tamati Waaka Nene, argued for acceptance, not of what would inevitably happen, but of what had already happened: 'Friends, whose potatoes do we eat? Whose were the blankets? . . . Is not the land already gone? Is it not covered, all covered with men, with strangers, with foreigners – even as the grass and weeds – over whom we have no power?' Turning to the British Resident, James Busby, he pleaded: 'Remain for us as a father, a judge, a peacemaker.' But the plea was conditional. 'You must not allow us to become slaves. You must preserve our customs and never let our land be taken from us.'

The Maori population continued to decline. In 1840 the native population had been estimated by missionaries and officials at being at least 100 000 – modern estimates put it considerably higher. The first reasonably accurate census, in 1857-8, calculated the Maori population at 56 000.

Some Maoris bowed to their fate, declining into fatalism and alcoholism. Others frantically tried to outplay the *pakeha* at their own game, farming ever larger acreages, building flour mills and acquiring fleets of coastal schooners. Others remained defiant and attempted the previously unthinkable – the creation of a single Maori nation. This was to be united under one ruler, complete with a flag, parliament and an official newspaper, *Te Hokioi*. Various battles ensued but, by 1870, the situation was secure enough for the last regiments of British regulars to be withdrawn.

By 1891 the Maori constituted just 7 per cent of the population. It was the low point of their relative weakness. But the succeeding century was to see them reclaim a place in their native land.

Within a century, a land that had once known only four mammals – bat, rat, dog and man – had acquired 80 000 horses, 400 000 cattle and 9 million sheep, not to mention the swarms of settlers who now outnumbered the natives by five to one.

INVADED NATION **A poor Maori family ekes a living from the soil, as the native population declines rapidly during the 19th century.**

THE FINAL FRONTIER

Europeans had been established at the Cape of Good Hope for
almost two centuries before they were impelled by their own conflicts to
launch an epic assault on the interior. Fleeing from British interference
in the simplicity of their traditional ways, the Voortrekkers uncovered
vast mineral wealth. This, in turn, simply encouraged the
unwelcome outsiders to invade their Promised Land.

THE END OF NOWHERE

Pioneers in other lands saw cities as symbols of progress

but the Boers shunned city life, viewing it as a source of evil and oppression,

and revelled instead in the emptiness of the veld.

THE BOERS eventually gained a reputation as colonisers of the veld, forever seeking better grazing beyond the next ridge. But this had not always been the case. Their Dutch ancestors had first settled at the Cape in 1652, valuing it only as a station on the sea route to spice-rich Indonesia, a pick-up point for 'herbs, flesh, water and other needful refreshments'. It was also a dumping-ground for those too sick to continue on to Batavia in Indonesia, or to survive the voyage back to Amsterdam – a proportion of crew and passengers which sometimes reached 50 per cent.

TEMPORARY HOMES The flimsy huts built by the native peoples of Natal were readily abandoned when better lands beckoned elsewhere.

The commander of the initial expedition of settlement was Jan van Riebeeck, a doctor by training. Far from intending the settlement to serve as a base for territorial expansion, the Dutch isolated part of the peninsula from the interior with a perimeter hedge, constructing watch-houses for defence purposes and marked out boundaries.

During the succeeding century, Cape Town grew into an imitation Dutch provincial city, with a jetty, fortress and church, white lime-washed houses, orchards and luxuriant gardens, peopled by elegantly dressed burghers. The white settlers were waited on by a large and varied underclass, which included native Africans, black slaves from Mozambique and Madagascar, imported Muslim Malays, Indians and Indonesians, poor white

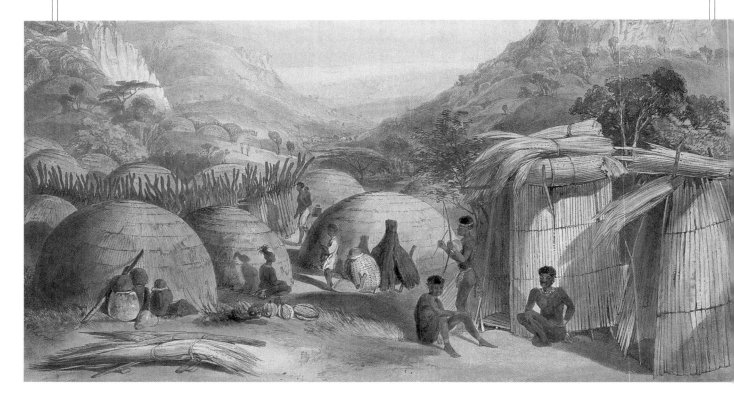

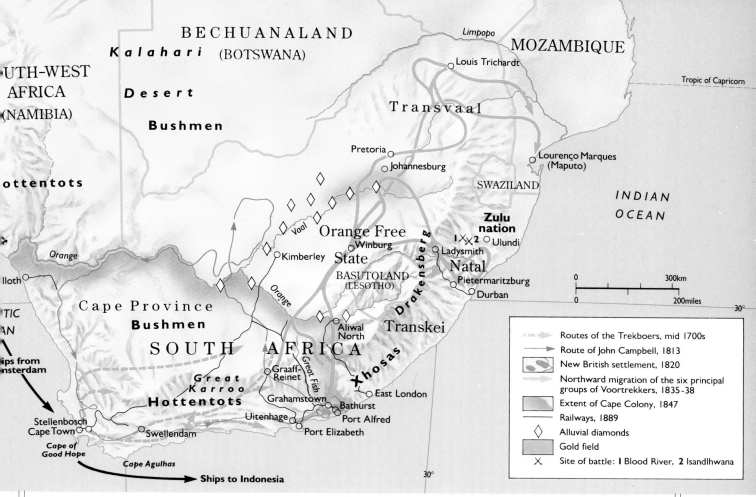

BECHUANALAND
(BOTSWANA)

Kalahari

Desert

Bushmen

SOUTH-WEST
AFRICA
(NAMIBIA)

Hottentots

Orange

Iloth

ATLANTIC
OCEAN

Ships from
Amsterdam

Cape Province
Bushmen

SOUTH   AFRICA

Great
Karroo
Hottentots

Stellenbosch
Cape Town

Cape of
Good Hope

Cape Agulhas

→ Ships to Indonesia

Limpopo

Louis Trichardt

MOZAMBIQUE

Transvaal

Tropic of Capricorn

Pretoria

Johannesburg

Lourenço Marques
(Maputo)

SWAZILAND

Zulu
nation

Ulundi

INDIAN
OCEAN

Orange Free

Winburg

Kimberley

State

BASUTOLAND
(LESOTHO)

Vaal

Orange

1 ╳╳ 2
Ladysmith

Natal

Pietermaritzburg

Durban

0   300km
0   200miles

30°

Aliwal
North

Transkei

Graaff-
Reinet

Grahamstown

Uitenhage

Swellendam

Great Fish

Xhosas

East London

Bathurst

Port Alfred

Port Elizabeth

30°

Drakensberg

Routes of the Trekboers, mid 1700s
Route of John Campbell, 1813
New British settlement, 1820
Northward migration of the six principal
groups of Voortrekkers, 1835-38
Extent of Cape Colony, 1847
Railways, 1889
Alluvial diamonds
Gold field
Site of battle: 1 Blood River, 2 Isandlhwana

SPREADING OUT South Africa's cities were initially clustered around the coast, reflecting the importance of continuing European contact. The later cities of the interior arose from the discovery of mineral wealth.

immigrants from the Netherlands and Germany, and even a few hundred Huguenot refugees. The European settlers were unquestioningly convinced of their superiority over the native races, and referred to native blacks as 'Kaffirs', a derogatory term derived from the Arabic for 'unbeliever'.

In one sense, the slaves were treated as members of their owner's family and they referred to the owner as 'father'. However, discipline was harsh and disobedience could be punished by savage flogging. The murder of an owner by his slave was construed as an act of patricide. The Swedish botanist, Carl Peter Thunberg, witnessed an example of retribution for such a crime in July 1773: 'The delinquent [was] laid on the cross and tied fast to it, first his arms and legs were burned in eight different parts with jagged tongs, made red hot; afterwards his arms and legs were broken on the wheel, and lastly, his head was cut off and fixed on a pole.'

All power – political and economic – was concentrated in the hands of the Dutch East India Company, the world's greatest trading corporation. Its local representatives – a tiny band of officials – were largely concerned with feathering their own nests. Compared with the inhabitants of the rural hinterland, the Cape Town elite were sophisticated; compared with their counterparts in the contemporary American

MULTIRACIAL SOCIETY
Immigrants came from Asia as well as Europe. Above: A man with a dog cart. Left: A Malay woman in European dress.

SPACE-SAVING **This Griqualand trekboer family of 1835 could be ready to move on within hours, quickly stowing their tent and stools to travel to wherever there was better grazing for their cattle.**

colonies, many of them were insular and ignorant. Such schools as there were, staffed by parish clerks in their spare time, provided only the most basic education. A high school, started in 1714 to offer Latin, gave up the unequal struggle and closed for lack of pupils within nine years. There was no local literature, painting, music or theatre. Not even the local company headquarters possessed a printing press, so there were no newspapers or journals. The only impressive buildings had been designed by European visitors, usually Dutch passing on to the East Indies. Cape Town was the only 'real' town in the entire colony. By 1795 it had 1145 houses, Stellenbosch had only 70, Swellendam 30, and Graaff Reinet consisted of barely a dozen mud huts.

LIFE FOR THE TREKBOER

The more adventurous of the colony's poor whites – who despised manual labour as the badge of bondage, but lacked the education to work for the Dutch East India Company or the capital to establish a vineyard or to keep an inn – saw a means of escape in the vast empty lands of the interior. There was a constant demand for meat, and for oxen to pull the wagons and ploughs. For a nominal annual payment to the company, they could graze an average of 6000 acres (2400 ha). Packing their families and their few possessions into huge ox-wagons they would trek into the unknown with their livestock and stop where the grazing seemed good. Trekboers, or graziers, were

TILLING THE EARTH **This early settler's plough is typical of those used by the Boers, a predominantly farming people.**

drawn from the Boer community, white South Africans born of Dutch parents. They usually considered everything within half an hour's gentle ride of wherever they stopped as being 'their' land, but would often only stay at each place for a few months. Unless or until they found a spot fertile enough to erect a makeshift 'house', made of mud walls and roofed with reeds, the ox-wagon would continue to serve as home.

Like many of the native pastoralists of South Africa, the Boers judged a man's wealth and standing not by his house but by his herds and the number of his sons and servants, who might total a dozen of the former and a hundred of the latter. What garrison commandant Ludwig Alberti, an employee of the Dutch East India Company, observed of the Bantu-speaking Xhosa in 1807 could equally well have been said of the Boer: 'The Kaffir's cattle is the foremost and practically the only subject of his care and occupation, in the possession of which he finds complete happiness.' Cattle were as central to the Boers' way of life as bison were to the Plains Indians of North America.

Meat was the staple of the trekboers' diet – grilled, fried, dried into chewy strips as biltong, or stewed with herbs and spices in recipes culled from the cuisines of Holland, Germany, France and Malaya. In their willingness to slaughter for the table, the trekboers differed from native herders who relied much more upon milk, *sorghum* (grass), beans and melons as staple items. They did not 'slaughter . . . cattle for food, except owing to sickness, old age or lameness . . . nor any sheep, except when two people get married'. In addition to their diet, trekboers also relied on their herds to provide them with the raw material for their footwear, garments, harnesses, buckets and tents. They even slept on beds made of wooden frames strung with

continued on page 134

A WANDERING MEESTER

ANDRIES REINED IN his horse, eased back in the saddle and stared down at the lush valley below. Beyond a massive herd of long-horned cattle grazing contentedly, he could see the thatched farm-house that was his destination.

He knew from long experience what to expect. On the *stoep*, or terraced verandah, there might be strong black coffee bubbling away, as well as a plate of crunchy rusks awaiting him. Outside, ox-skulls would serve as seats, with hide-covered stools inside. The clay-floored interior would have open corner cupboards for crockery, wooden crates for storage, a chest for valuables, and a butter churn. Freshly slaughtered meat would be suspended from the rafters and, perhaps, hanging on the wall, a fearsome *sjambok* (whip), woven from hippopotamus hide.

In the evening, there would be plenty to eat and drink, and a smouldering fire of dried cow dung

CRACK SHOT **The hat worn by the Boer huntsman in this drawing sheltered his eyes in the shimmering heat.**

or mimosa thorn wood. The meal would be the same as breakfast – stewed meat with bread or rice, followed by soup with flour dumplings. Although it was stodgy, simple fare, there was always

plenty of it. Not even the Boers' worst enemies could deny that they were hospitable, even to a passing stranger.

Andries was a nomad among nomads. Since he had lost his own family from fever, and most of his herd from drought, he had traded on his slender education to live as a wandering *meester*, or teacher, attaching himself to one family after another, sometimes for weeks, sometimes for years. They needed him, not because educa-tion was considered essential for success in business, but because a basic acquaintance with the Bible and Church dogma was necessary before a boy could offer himself for *aangenomen* (confirmation) – a prerequisite for marriage. Andries' halting literacy and patchy knowl-edge of the Old Testament won him superficial respect from stout-hearted farmers and their *vrouwen* (wives).

Andries won even greater respect when they learned that he had ridden with many a *commando* (mili-tary expedition) against cattle raiders and had proved himself to be a fine horseman and an excel-lent shot. There was always room for such a man among an embat-tled people.

GAME HUNT **A group of Boers return on horseback from a hunt. As well as providing the Boers with pleasure, the game they shot provided a high proportion of their meat-rich diet.**

CAPE TOWN

CAPE TOWN after a generation of British rule was still visibly a meeting-point between the simplicity of frontier life and the sophistication of an imperial power. The neatly aligned street of multi-storey buildings, with bow windows, porticoes and a raised sidewalk, contrasts with the dust or mud of the broad shapeless street and the rural character of the open-air market selling farm-fresh produce. Bourgeois couples parade in the current European fashions, while up-country Boers trundle past in their ox-drawn carts. The bright uniforms of the military are a constant reminder of the semi-permanent state of warfare along the inland frontier and the ultimate sanction behind colonial government. In 1840, Cape Town, with a population of 20 000, was granted the status of a municipality. For administrative purposes it was divided into 12 districts, each headed by an elected commissioner.

DIVISION OF LABOUR   In this painting by Thomas Baines, black servants wait on a Boer family.

riempies (rawhide thongs), and in place of ropes used *riems* (leather strips) to tether their beasts. The trekboers would usually return to the Cape once a year to renew their licence and to sell the increase of their herds, as well as goods they had made from by-products of the cattle such as soap, butter, candles and tallow, and ivory from the elephants they had shot. The money that they made paid for the few essentials which they could not produce for themselves, such as coffee, tea, sugar, rice and spices; powder and shot for their long-barrelled flintlock muskets; raw

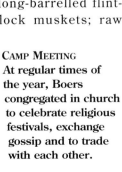

CAMP MEETING
At regular times of the year, Boers congregated in church to celebrate religious festivals, exchange gossip and to trade with each other.

materials such as iron and pitch; and, more rarely, such luxuries as a pewter plate or bowl, or a length of Flemish linen. These exchanges were usually the limit of their contact with the so-called civilised world – and that was how they liked it. Some never left the veld, relying on pedlars – often former soldiers or sailors – to sell them what they needed and to buy their livestock from them.

Each year the trekboers would push the frontier a little farther forward, following the courses of great rivers and probing for passes through the formidable mountains which protected the high plateaus of the interior. In the 1750s – a century after the first Dutch settlement at Cape Town – the inhabitants of the port still looked to the oceans for their prosperity and to Europe for culture. But the trekboers had by now penetrated almost 500 miles (800 km) inland and were scattered over an area twice the size of England.

The Boers distrusted governments and hated taxes. The constitutional historian James Bryce (1838-1922) observed that they were 'individualistic to excess . . . and little disposed to brook the control even of the authorities they had themselves created'. They had, he concluded, what amounted to 'a genius for disobedience'. Fiercely clannish,

WOMEN'S LIBERATION AMONG THE BOERS

THE FEMINIST writer Olive Schreiner (1855-1920) wanted to provoke her readers with her essay *The Boer Woman and the Modern Woman's Question*, written in 1890. She believed that Boer women had already achieved sexual equality due to their equal rights to property, their equal access to education and their uncomplicated attitude to marriage: ❝ "I am sick of all this talk of choosing and choosing," says the old-fashioned mother, whose children may have imbibed somewhat of the modern attitude on the subject. "If a man is healthy and does not drink, and has a good little handful of stock and good temper, and is a good Christian, what great difference can it make to a woman which man she takes? There is not so much difference between one man and another." . . . We know of few social conditions in which the duties and enjoyments of life are so equally divided between the sexes, none in which they are more so. This assuredly is no small matter . . . If the Boer woman still sits motionless in her elbow-chair today, when her sisters of the Old World and the New are rising to their feet to readjust their relation to life – she yet does well to sit there till her conditions of life change, for it is a throne. ❞

the Boers desired not only independence but isolation – large towns made them uneasy, and they much preferred space, freedom and hunting. They were African, born and bred, and of Europe and its heritage they knew little and cared less. The Dutch they spoke was already evolving into a distinctive tongue – Afrikaans – with a much simplified grammar and a vocabulary which incorporated bits of French, Malay and Portuguese, as well as borrowings from traditional African languages.

The isolation of life on the veld was broken four times a year by the celebration of Holy Communion, which became, in effect, a small fair, attracting pedlars and horse-traders. Families in their ox-wagons would converge on the chosen site. Those with relatives nearby would lodge with them and swap family news, while the rest pitched their tents. The wagon-shed of a centrally placed farm would serve to house the service. As time passed, a favoured site might become the nucleus of a tiny *dorp* (village) with a store for a *smous* – someone who might also act as postmaster and letter-writer – and a hall which could double as a church and schoolhouse. Later, a few of the wealthier members of the congregation might build houses and contribute to the construction of a proper church with a full-time *predikant* (pastor). But even these mini-villages were slow to grow. Two centuries after van Riebeeck's arrival, there

WANDERING HERDSMAN The nomadic Khoikhoi tribe often traded with the Boers, who gave them the name 'Hottentots'.

were only 45 dorps, most of which were in the Cape region. As late as 1921, the number had still only reached 369.

THE KILLING FIELDS

The Boers' invasion of the interior was inevitably contested by others who laid claim to the use of the land. There were the yellow-skinned herders of cattle and fat-tailed sheep who called themselves Khoikhoi – 'men of men' – and whom the Boers referred to as Hottentots. The Khoikhoi were often willing to trade with the Boers, exchanging livestock or *mealies* (maize) for beads of copper or glass, tobacco or brandy. Copper – in wire or sheet form – was especially valued, used almost exclusively to make such items of personal adornment as bracelets, necklaces, rings, anklets, crowns, bells, amulets and hair ornaments.

Sometimes Khoikhoi would work for the Boers as herdsmen, labourers or cooks, receiving their keep and often the right to graze small herds of their own on inferior land. This was even less generous than it seemed, since owners of livestock were less likely to try to abscond. At times mutual cattle-raiding between Boers and Khoikhoi was endemic, in which case Khoikhoi might be found on opposing sides, for many were trusted with horses and guns by the Boers to serve on punitive commando expeditions. With the Bushmen, however, there was no such exchange. These non-Bantu speakers were ethnically distinct, and lived by hunting and gathering in the deserts and mountains, rather than by herding or farming in the lowlands. Whenever they could, the Bushmen raided Boer herds, regarding them as another form of game, albeit conveniently collected together. In retribution, the Boers killed the Bushmen, sparing only their children, so that they could become 'apprentices'. In one ten-year period, Boer commandos killed some 2500 people and carried off more than 600 of their children as captives. The commando, which began as an instrument of defence, thus became a mechanism for acquiring labour.

By the mid 18th century, the Boers had spread through the eastern Cape and had

FIGHTING BACK Above: Escaped Khoikhoi shelter in a cave. Below: Khoikhoi raiders drive a stolen herd into their mountain fastness and prepare an ambush for the pursuing Boers.

also begun to come into intermittent contact with the Xhosa, a Bantu-speaking people who lived as pastoralists, involved in trading or raiding as the opportunities arose. When they fought the Xhosa – whose name is Khoikhoi for 'angry men' – the Boers found them more formidable than any other encountered by a commando.

Full-scale warfare between Boer and Bantu began in 1779-81 and recurred spasmodically throughout the succeeding century, depending on where the line was drawn between a raid and a campaign. The conflicts were bloody and bitter, but not without chivalry. Xhosa warriors did not kill women and children, and even respected the pacifism of missionaries. Boer commandos also spared women and children because they could enslave them for their much-valued breeding power and labour. During the earliest encounters the Xhosa often held their own, but in later conflicts the whites ruthlessly burnt to the ground their crops and huts, destroying their food supplies and forcing them to yield land or starve. As on other frontiers on other continents, the native peoples were more numerous and fought bravely but they were divided by ethnic rivalries and handicapped by inferior arms.

'GOD'S CHOSEN PEOPLE'
Warfare hardly troubled Boer consciences, for their reading of the Bible assured them of the inherent superiority of the white man over the black, the Christian over the Kaffir. A British writer who had lived among the Boers for a decade wrote in 1871 that: 'They have persuaded themselves by some wonderful mental process that they are God's chosen people, and that the blacks are the wicked and condemned Canaanites over whose heads the divine anger lowers continually.'

In 1876 the wife of a French missionary was informed by a Boer policeman that: 'If by any accident a Kaffir, even one, were to be seen in Heaven when he (the policeman) got there, he would pick up his hat and wish the Almighty goodbye and walk straight out.' The same author noted that

HALF-CASTE **An alliance with the British helped the mixed-race Griquas to preserve a measure of autonomy. The Boers called the Griquas 'Bastaards'.**

SUBTLE DIFFERENCES

Livestock were so important to the way of life of African pastoralists that they developed a large and subtle vocabulary to describe them. The Mpondo people had at least 57 different terms for as many markings, and five more for various types of horns.

many Boers clung obstinately to the belief that the Earth was flat.

The Boers' sense of superiority did not, however, prevent them from having occasional recourse to African diviners and herbalists. Nor did it stand in the way of concubinage, although formal marriage between the races had been banned as early as 1685. Sexual relationships led to the formation of yet another distinctive ethnic group – half-castes, the ancestors of today's 'Cape Coloured' community. As they were usually disowned by their white fathers, they were bluntly known as 'Bastaards'. Some entered Boer service and became, in effect, serfs, like many Khoikhoi who had lost their land and cattle. Others retreated beyond the frontier to lead a Boer-like existence, attracting to their numbers runaway slaves, white criminals, refugees from tribal wars, and other misfits. One branch of these people were described in 1812 as 'Bastard-Hottentots . . . clothed after the European manner . . . converts to Christianity', who 'lived by breeding cattle, or by the chase . . . and . . . obtained powder and ball . . . by a traffic in elephants' teeth'. In 1813 the missionary John Campbell persuaded them that, instead of blithely accepting the designation of 'Bastaards', they should adopt something less offensive. The African side of their ancestry led them naturally to think in terms of lineage: 'On consulting among themselves, they found the majority were descended from a person of the name of Griqua, and they resolved hereafter to be called Griquas.'

Khoikhoi and half-castes alike were relentlessly driven ever farther from the coast by the Boers. Campbell recorded in 1813 that 'an old Hottentot told us that he remembered the time

FIRST LANDING In Thomas Baines's painting, British settlers arrive in Algoa Bay in 1820.

THOMAS BAINES (1822-75) served a five-year apprenticeship as an ornamental painter in Norfolk, decorating the coaches of the gentry with their coats of arms. But, eager for adventure, the 20-year-old Baines set off for South Africa. At first he made a living painting ships and seascapes, but in 1848 he moved to Grahamstown in the interior. From there he ventured into the surrounding bush, making sketches in the field and working them up into finished oil paintings back at Grahamstown.

In 1851, Baines was invited to accompany British forces during the Eighth Frontier War, thus becoming South Africa's first war artist. After two years of painting, sketching – and fighting – he was back in Britain, lecturing about his exploits. Soon, the prospect of further adventures tempted Baines abroad again; in 1855 he joined an expedition to northern Australia, combining the roles of official artist and storekeeper. Baines's courage, cheerfulness, integrity and skill as a cartographer so impressed his employers that Mount Baines was named in his honour, and a special commendation of his efforts was issued by the colonial government. In 1857 the Royal Geographical Society elected him a Fellow and helped to secure his appointment as artist/storekeeper to accompany the Scottish missionary-explorer David Livingstone up the Zambezi in 1858. It was a venture that proved disastrous for Baines, who was unjustly accused of pilfering from stores. Amid bitter mutual recriminations, he left the expedition. In 1861 Baines accompanied the hunter James Chapman on a journey of exploration from present-day Namibia, inland as far as the Victoria Falls. This formed the basis of his *Explorations in Southwest Africa*, published in 1864 and illustrated with coloured lithographs. His fame and fortune established, Baines opened a London studio in 1865 and co-authored a practical handbook for explorers, called *Shifts and Expedients of Camp Life*. He returned to Africa again in 1872, when he organised expeditions to look for gold in Matabeleland, southern Rhodesia. Baines was a poor businessman and had to churn out canvases to pay off debts incurred by his costly forays into the interior.

Baines died of dysentery at Durban, aged 53, while planning yet another expedition. Two years after his death, the illustrations, scientific data and accurate maps that he had accumulated in Matabeleland were published together as *The Gold Regions of South-Eastern Africa*.

when the Boers were all within five days' journey of Cape Town, and the country was full of Hottentot kraals (compounds filled with huts); but they have been gradually driven up the country to make room for the white people'.

ARRIVAL OF THE BRITISH

At the time Campbell was writing, the Boers had a new and even stronger reason to distance themselves from Cape Town and the authority it represented – the arrival of the British.

The British took control of the Cape in 1806 as a by-product of the Napoleonic Wars. Like the Dutch before them, they valued it primarily for its location – en route to India, and later to Singapore and Hong Kong. The possibility that it might contain hidden wealth was, at the time of annexation, unsuspected. The only real interest the British had in the frontier was to stabilise it. For this purpose, Parliament subsidised the colony to the tune of £50 000 and in 1820 imported 4000 settlers. The intention was that they should become small farmers in the Zuurveld region, along the western side of the Great Fish River, and constitute a human barrier against further native African incursions.

The settlers were less than ideal pioneering stock – more than half were 'broken tradesmen' and 'disappointed artisans'. A fair proportion of the remainder were relatively well-to-do families whose idea of rural living meant a country mansion where

SIMPLE STYLE Although sparsely furnished, the affluence of this wealthy settler home is indicated by the wall portraits and abundant glassware.

they could hunt, fish and be waited on by docile servants. Three successive harvest failures, followed by disastrous floods in 1823, led all but 600 of the immigrants to abandon the areas assigned to them and to seek employment in the towns of Grahamstown and Port Elizabeth.

Those who did stay eventually made good, when the introduction of merino sheep led to wool becoming Cape Colony's chief export. By the 1860s it accounted for 73 per cent of total export values. Angora goats from Turkey, which thrived on tough scrub unsuitable for sheep, were imported and in less than 20 years Cape Colony was exporting more mohair from Angoran goats than the Turkish province of Angora itself. The domestication of the native ostrich began around 1860 and soon 'proved to be a very interesting and highly remunerative pursuit', providing European ladies with flamboyant fans and dramatic decoration for their millinery.

British rule meant better roads, the creation of postal and telegraph services, new churches, schools and libraries, recourse to regular courts of law with juries, and a revolution in urban life thanks to such novelties as banks, retail shops, newspapers, debating societies, racecourses and cricket matches. Manufactured goods became

FRONTIER TOWN Grahamstown, shown here in 1823, was founded in 1812 by Colonel George Graham as a frontier stronghold against the Xhosa.

By Rail from the Cape to Johannesburg

SOUTH AFRICA acquired railways late but, once built, their comfort and efficiency impressed contemporaries, as the author of *The Gold Fields of South Africa* (1890) was at pains to make clear:

❝ The visitor will observe that the Railway accommodation provided is in no way inferior to that of the home Railways, and that the comfort of the passenger is much better attended to . . . The carriages are long vehicles, built somewhat after the American "Pullman" type, with some having separate compartments and a continuous covered-passage; the ends forming covered platforms for smoking or enjoying the varied scenery . . . no expense has been spared to make them as comfortable as possible, a special feature being the sleeping bunks which . . . can be adjusted . . . enabling four passengers to sleep in each compartment. The train is shortly to be lighted by the electric light; a kitchen car is attached, and meals are served in a style worthy of a first class hotel . . . Lavatories are also provided . . . The journey – from Cape Town to Johannesburg – occupies 31¾ hours. We select the fast train which leaves Cape Town weekly after the arrival of the Mail Steamer. The spacious station . . . presents an animated appearance . . . [Some] are seasoned colonists who have made the journey a score of times . . . others are strangers just arrived . . . anxious to see that their baggage is fairly divided between their smoking carriage and the guard's van. The bell clangs, the engine shrieks, there is a shaking of hands outstretched from the carriage windows, a waving of hats, and the train starts on its 650 mile [1050 km] journey. ❞

more plentiful but remained dear, relative to the price of food and drink. As late as 1860, a jacket could cost a skilled craftsman two days' wages; for the same money he could buy 2 gallons (9 litres) of brandy.

As English became the favoured medium of government, law and commerce, English-speaking newcomers had a powerful incentive to keep themselves apart from the Afrikaners. However, many Britons – particularly in rural areas – came to accept and perpetuate the traditional Boer attitude to race – that the native black population were condemned by history and theology alike to remain hewers of wood and drawers of water in their own land. They believed that freedom for native peoples amounted to an endorsement of barbarism, as *The Graham's Town Journal* thundered in 1843: 'It is sheer folly to talk of the RIGHT of any people to maintain among themselves usages which are not only positively immoral, but which are manifestly injurious to their neighbours . . . We tell the British Government, for the hundredth time, that it is an utter absurdity to expect the barbarous natives on the borders of this Colony to become civilised until

SLAVERY OVERTURNED   A procession with drums and flags marks the abolition of slavery in the 1830s.

MEETING POINT In a sparsely populated land, the canteen (tavern) was somewhere for the far-flung settlers to gather.

they are placed under proper government, or, in other words, wholesome control.'

The British authorities, however, were under pressure from a powerful missionary and anti-slavery lobby in Britain itself. This triumphed in the 1830s, when Parliament decreed the formal abolition of slavery throughout the Empire, and that included Cape Colony.

Worse still for the racist, was the appointment of officials and the establishment of legal procedures to ensure minimal rights of personal security, property and fair treatment to the nonwhite population. To the Boer this placing of slaves 'on an equal

footing with Christians [was] contrary to the laws of God and the natural distinctions of race and religion, so that it was intolerable for any decent Christian to bow down beneath such a yoke'.

THE GREAT TREK

To preserve their racial and cultural identity, the Boers decided to move beyond the rule of the British, taking with them a roughly equal number of their 'servants' and 'apprentices'. Between 1835 and 1843, this exodus deprived the eastern Cape of almost a fifth of its entire white population.

The aim of these *Voortrekkers* – 'forward journeyers' – was to re-create in the far distant interior a new Afrikaner society, where it would be possible to 'preserve proper relations between master and servant'. The first parties to leave, in 1835, paid the highest price for their daring, with one group wiped out by native Tsonga warriors; the other lost many of its people to malaria, and most of its cattle to the tsetse fly. Four large parties left in 1836-7. The first two penetrated to the high Veld only to find themselves faced by a huge force of Ndebele

---

LATE DEVELOPERS

The European settlement of America began in 1607, and that of South Africa in 1652. By 1870, southern Africa had only 69 miles (111 km) of railway and a white population of 250 000. The United States had 53 000 miles (85 300 km) of railways and a white population of 32 000 000.

141

HAND-TO-HAND Heavily outnumbered, the Voortrekkers tried to use their firepower to keep the Zulu enemy at bay and to avoid one-to-one fighting. This painting shows a Zulu attack during the Great Trek.

warriors, a sub-group of the Zulu. Forming their wagons into a *laager* (a defensive ring), reinforced with thorn scrub, they drove off their attackers, who suffered huge losses. Although the Voortrekkers had few casualties, they lost all their herds; a southward retreat to join up with column leader Gert Maritz's later party enabled them to acquire fresh livestock. The combined parties elected a *Krygsraad* (Council of War) and took their revenge early in 1837, heading straight for the 'Great Place' – the Ndebele capital. When the Ndebele unwisely adopted their traditional tactic of offering combat in a close-packed formation, they were shattered by a punitive commando of 140 men, who raked them with concentrated firepower. Rejoicing, the victors returned with 7000 head of cattle.

In September 1837 the Voortrekkers split into two groups, the majority opting to continue north to Transvaal, the smaller group heading east into Natal. Descending from the Drakensberg Mountains, this small group found lush pastures which must have seemed like the promised land they sought. Initial contacts with the Zulu chief Dingane encouraged them to believe that he would accept them as neighbours. When the Voortrekkers' gifted leader, Piet Retief, visited Dingane's *kraal* to ratify their agreement, he and his hundred-strong escort were tricked into abandoning their arms as a gesture of courtesy. Retief and his men were overpowered, bound, and clubbed to death. Zulu *impis*, or regiments, sent against the Voortrekker camps, then killed another 500 pioneers.

The survivors took their revenge. On a bright Sunday morning in December 1838, at a bend in the Ncome river, an expeditionary column of 468 Voortekkers, armed with rifles and three small

cannon, formed a *laager*, protected on one side by the river and on another by a deep gully. Against them came 15 000 Zulus. For two hours, wave after wave of Zulus hurled themselves against point-blank volleys of fire. Then, as the Zulus faltered, Commandant-General Andries Pretorius (in whose honour Pretoria was named) ordered a daring series of cavalry charges, the third of which split the Zulu army, driving them into the river or the gully. Every warrior who took refuge in the gully was slaughtered. So many took refuge in the reeds that the river Ncome ran red with their blood (hence the name, the Battle of Blood River). At least 3000 Zulus died in the conflict, with only three Boers injured.

Ironically, this victory did not guarantee the Boers' possession of their new Eden. Five years

EPIC ENCOUNTER A Zulu warrior (left) prepares for combat. Below: At the Battle of Blood River, the Boers formed their wagons into a defensive *laager*, or ring.

SPOILS OF THE CHASE Its sheer power and ferocity made the rhinoceros a formidable hunting quarry for the settlers. Left: African wildlife, such as the giraffe, became a big attraction in European zoos.

later the British annexed Natal, and most of the Boers retreated over the Drakensberg to rejoin their brethren on the highveld.

Once the Voortrekkers had consolidated their hold on the lands to be found beyond the Orange and Vaal rivers, the British grudgingly agreed to recognise the Orange Free State and the South African Republic (Transvaal) as autonomous entities in the 1850s.

However, the much-cherished remoteness of the Voortrekkers also came with its price – postriders carrying the mail for Cape Colony and abroad had to leave Bloemfontein by four o'clock in the afternoon to avoid danger from the wildlife, particularly the lions, which lurked around the fringes of the 'capital'.

As the Boers penetrated the interior, so the British moved into Natal, which was formally annexed in 1843. Five thousand British immigrants arrived between 1849 and 1852 alone. A few years later came veterans of the German Legion which had fought in the British army during the Crimean War.

ENVIRONMENTAL DESTRUCTION

Meeting the everyday needs of these new settlers sparked off an environmental revolution, which changed the local ecology more in three decades than the African farmers had done in 15 centuries. Natal's Surveyor-General estimated that even a family of six – small by the standards of the day – used about a ton-and-a-half of firewood a month. There was an additional commercial demand from the manufacturers of bricks, candles, soap and sugar. Higher grades of wood were needed by carpenters, coopers (barrel-makers) and the makers of furniture, wagons and boats. As early as 1853, any settler who wanted to cut timber on Crown land had to pay a licence fee of £1 per month per saw. Durban resident John Sanderson noted that within 15 years 'the demand for timber has caused

NATURE'S SACRIFICE   Ivory from elephant tusks was made into piano keys, knife handles, combs, jewellery, and even false teeth. Below: Ostriches were one of a range of tropical birds hunted for their plumage, to grace the hats of European ladies.

all the larger trees near the town to be cut down . . . The Red Mangrove is so highly valued for posts, stakes and other such outdoor purposes, that few trees of any size are now to be found in the Bay of Natal. . . .' By the 1860s timber had been used up so far inland that it was already cheaper to import deal wood from America or the Baltic than to haul it to the coast from the interior.

The settlers' impact on local wildlife was no less dramatic. One family of ten, who ran a large sugar estate, kept two of their six sons employed full-time in hunting to supply the house-hold with meat. In a single month in 1864, a farmer near the foothills of the Drakensberg mountains recorded that he had shot 17 buck and 46 brace of birds, just for his own larder. In their early years, families struggling to estab-lish themselves as farmers relied heavily on game, such as pigeon, bustard and buck, until they could vary their diet with their own poultry, bacon and mutton.

The best hunters made a good living supplying European traders with such exotic goods as ivory,

hides, horns and ostrich feathers, and live speci-mens for natural history societies and zoos. Agents placed advertisements in the local Press requesting, among other species, wildebeest, hartebeest, eland, buffalo, eagles and herons. Some creatures, notably lions and leopards, were hunted down as a menace to life and livestock, as well as the crocodiles which haunted unbridged river crossings. In 1866 a Noxious Animals Law positively encouraged the destruction of leopards, hyenas and jackals. In the same year, a clique of sportsmen persuaded the Legislative Council to pass a law protecting their favourite quarry – buck, buffalo, ostrich, partridge, pheasant and guinea-fowl. Unintentional decima-tion of wildlife was caused by effluent from sugar mills, which killed shoals of fish in the Umhlanga River as early as the 1870s. The drainage of large swamps around Durban eliminated the feeding-ground of snipe and wild duck. By 1870 eland, leopard, ostrich and buffalo in coastal Natal were rare; but lion, elephant and rhinoceros were nowhere to be seen.

JOHANNESBURG – CITY OF GOLD
The uneasy stand-off between Briton and Boer was shattered with the discovery of diamonds along the Orange and Vaal rivers in 1867, and of gold on the

Witwatersrand (White Waters Ridge) in 1886. From an economic backwater, southern Africa became a magnet for immigrants and the crucible of the continent's first industrial revolution. Before the discovery of gold in 1886, the area now covered by Johannesburg was simply farmland. It is the only major South African city which is not located on a river, a lake shore or the coast.

A grid pattern of narrow streets was laid out in 1886, and the telegraph office and Stock Exchange were opened a year later. The city's first local authority was the Goldfield Diggers Committee – thus revealing its most urgent priority. Within less than three years, the city had a white, largely English-speaking, population of 25 000, plus an uncounted black population of labourers, drivers, pedlars and beggars. By 1892 Johannesburg was at last linked by rail to Cape Town, 800 miles (1290 km) away. By 1894 it had acquired a telephone link to the rest of the country. The English historian

ON THE MOVE   Left: A migrant makes his way to the goldfields. Below: A black family passes a road-marker 30 miles (48 km) from Grahamstown. Paid work would enable such families to return to the interior with rifles, cloth and cooking pots.

A Diamond-Field Doctor: Latrines and Lacerations

For Posterity Diamond miners and their families pose for a photograph beside their 'diggings' near Kimberley.

CHARLIE FREEMAN peered out through the flaps of his tent. He grunted at the grey-pink dawn and motioned to the half-caste girl – who served him as cook, washerwoman and nursing assistant – to bring him coffee. Turning back into the tent, he looked down at his patient, a bearded ex-farmer with a badly gashed arm. Charlie was confident that there was no danger of infection. Nevertheless, he would tell the man to return every few days so that he could change the dressing and check on the progress of the wound's healing. The men never took time off to convalesce; only the severest pain or illness would keep a prospector from his sieves and sorting table.

No one could say that his medical practice lacked variety. As a fully qualified physician, unlike the many self-styled 'doctors' who frequented most mining camps, Charlie was paid by the authorities to act as a part-time sanitary inspector. Thus, the first call on his time in the morning would be a stroll through the areas set aside for latrines and then a walk around the market to ensure that none of the traders was trying to sell rotten goods.

In the heat of the day, he would make his 'house calls', chiefly checking on pregnant women, and children down with the usual ailments. Most of the men came in the evening when it was too dark to work. A real emergency would, however, find him quickly on the spot, summoned by a signal of three gunshots fired in succession.

As the only trained medical man within a 20 mile (32 km) radius of the diggings, Charlie could charge pretty much what he liked for both treatment and medicines. However, he never abused his power and had been pleasantly surprised at the promptness with which the miners settled their bills, often paying in small precious stones rather than cash. Having no professional colleagues nearby to whom he could refer a patient, Charlie had, in six months, progressed far beyond the normal bread-and-butter work of bandaging and bonesetting.

Although the light was fading, Charlie could make out the figure of a man approaching, with his hand clutched to his jaw in pain. Rummaging among his tools for a pair of dental pincers, Charlie called his assistant to fetch a three-legged stool and the jug of fierce Cape brandy which served as an anaesthetic for extractions.

INSTANT CITY Johannesburg did not exist in 1886 – but by 1902 it had a population of approximately 100 000.

James Bryce visited Johannesburg in 1897 and found it 'a busy, eager, restless, pleasure-loving town'. In that same year the Sanitary Committee attained the dignity of a Town Council. But most of the white population, being English-speaking *uitlanders* (foreigners), were excluded from the vote by the Boers.

Their discontent helped to precipitate the Anglo-Boer War of 1899-1902, which was accompanied by

a flight of English-speakers from the city. Control of the gold fields was a prime strategic objective for the British and they captured Johannesburg, with its mines undamaged, in 1900. When the war ended, the labour shortage in the mines was so acute, even though the city's population was by now 100 000, that Chinese workers were drafted in, although they were all repatriated by 1910. The British novelist John Buchan described the boom city: 'An extended brickfield is the first impression: a prosperous powder-factory is the last. . . .'

Between 1875 and 1904, immigration more than tripled the white population of southern Africa. Investment poured into the region to provide the capital equipment for deep-mining precious metals and gems, and to build railways to link the vast heartland with the coast and thus with global commerce. In 1870 there had been only 69 miles (111 km) of railway in the whole of the region, British or Boer; by 1886 there were 1800 miles (2900 km), and Cape Town was joined to Kimberley. By 1895 the figure had doubled again, and Johannesburg was now linked to Port Elizabeth, East London, Durban and even Lourenço Marques in Portuguese East Africa.

INDIAN IMMIGRANTS Cheap labour was initially imported from the western areas of India to cultivate the cash crops of Natal.

Meanwhile, Britain took over more and more tribal territories, frustrating Boer efforts to secure an independent outlet to the sea. The Boer republics eventually fought to resist the avalanche of greed and technology which swept over their retreat.

THE BOER WAR

The Boers severely dented British military pride. Superior numbers and firepower made the eventual outcome inevitable, but the cost was high. During the war of 1899-1902 the British had to mobilise an army of 450 000 men and suffer 22 000 fatalities to defeat Boer forces totalling 88 000.

However, with southern Africa supplying a third of the world's gold and more than half of its diamonds, there was too much at stake for Britain not to pay the price of victory, however high.

MARCHING AS TO WAR Transvaal burghers pause to pose on their way to the war front in a commandeered commercial vehicle.

BOER WAR TACTICS

To defeat the Boers during the war of 1899-1902, British forces burned 30 000 farms and forced Afrikaner civilians to live in inefficiently administered 'concentration' camps, where 28 000 – mostly children – died of dysentery and measles. The British also built 8000 blockhouses to guard the railways and 3700 miles (6000 km) of barbed-wire fences to isolate Boer guerrillas.

Peace was achieved when the Boer republics of Transvaal and Orange River Colony were embodied in the British Empire, and the remaining Boers laid down their arms. In 1910 Briton and Boer found themselves joined together in South Africa – a new dominion seeking a new future. There were no longer any 'empty lands' or frontiers to relieve the frictions of their coexistence. Now they would have to learn to live together.

TIME CHART

WORLD EVENTS

1703 Colony of Delaware founded.

1709 First mass emigration of Germans to America.

1713 France cedes Newfoundland to Britain.

1714 George I becomes king.

1720 The British South Sea Trading Company speculation collapses.

1727 George II succeeds to throne.

1729 Baltimore founded.

1733 Georgia, last of the Thirteen Colonies, is founded.

1735 French found first settlement in Indiana.

1749 Halifax, Nova Scotia founded.

BY STEALTH Boats with muffled oars land British troops to seize Quebec, and with it Canada.

1759 British defeat French at Quebec.

1760 George III succeeds to throne.

GUIDE Daniel Boone leads pioneers through the Cumberland Gap in the Appalachian Mountains, USA.

1763 Peace of Paris confirms British ascendancy in Canada and India.

1769 Captain Cook discovers Australia and lands in New Zealand.

1773 Boston Tea Party.

Cook becomes the first person to cross the Antarctic Circle.

LEISURE AND LEARNING

1701 Yale College founded.

1710 Four Iroquois chiefs visit London.

1727 The first Roman Catholic Mission established in Minnesota.

1732 Ninepins introduced to New York.

1734 First horse-race to take place in America is held at Charleston

HORSE-RACING Racing over a measured track in 1734. The jockeys' weigh-in scales are also shown.

Neck, South Carolina.

1746 Princeton founded as the 'College of New Jersey'.

1752 Benjamin Franklin invents the lightning rod.

BOOKS
Cotton Mather's *Magnalia Christi Americana* (1702); *The Redeemed Captive* by John Williams (1707); *Robinson Crusoe* by Daniel Defoe (1719).

THEATRE AND MUSIC
1752 First theatre in USA built in Philadelphia; Lewis Hallam arrives in USA from England with a troupe of actors, marking the beginning of the professional theatre in America.

1766 First play about American Indians, *Ponteach, or The Savages of America* written by Robert Rogers.

LIFESTYLE CHANGES

SECONDHAND A London street-seller of used clothes. Clothes were often handed down through the family.

1709 Regular monthly postal service between Bristol and New York started.

1719 German immigrants arrive in Louisiana.

1720 Swiss immigrants introduce rifles to American colonies.

1721 Smallpox inoculation gives early settlers in North America immunity, but native populations are

not protected.

1727 Coffee first planted in Brazil.

1730 Freemasons' Lodge founded in Philadelphia.

1749 First settlement west of the Alleghenies established at Marlinton.

1752 First European settlement in Arizona.

1754 Canadian fur trappers reach the Rockies. Beaver skins become basic unit of currency in the west; a fashion for beaver-skin hats develops in Europe.

1760 Daniel Boone scouts sites for settlement in Tennessee.

1763 The Jesuits expelled from Louisiana.

British Government forbids settlement west of the Appalachians.

1769 Spanish settlers introduce wheat, wine and oranges to California.

Jean de Surville gives hogs to Maori chief, urging him to breed them.

1773 Cook plants first potatoes in New Zealand and gives Maoris a pig. Potatoes flourish and hogs multiply, providing good food sources for both settlers and natives.

1774 'Mother Ann' Lee Stanley, Shaker prophetess, emigrates to America from England.

TRADE WITHOUT WORDS One of Captain Cook's sailors barters with a native to trade in his cloth for a tasty crustacean.

1776 American Declaration of Independence.

1779 Captain Cook killed in Hawaii.

1780 London devastated by anti-Catholic Gordon riots.

1781 Los Angeles is recognised as a settlement.

1783 Pitt the Younger becomes Prime Minister of Britain at the age of 24.

1784 Russia establishes first colony in Alaska.

1787 United States adopts a new constitution.

1788 'First fleet' of convict ships arrives at Botany Bay, Australia.

RULING CLASS Earl Macartney (1737-1806) became the first British Governor of Cape Town.

1789 French issue Declaration of the Rights of Man.

The *Bounty* mutineers settle in the Pitcairn islands.

1801-3 Matthew Flinders circumnavigates Australia.

1806 British capture Cape Town.

1807 Britain abolishes slave trade.

1812-15 War between USA and Britain; British burn Washington.

1789 First maps of American roads published.

1792 Construction of the White House and the Capitol Building begins in Washington.

1794 Eli Whitney invents the cotton gin.

1797 Cast-iron plough patented in US.

1800 The first upright pianos are manufactured in Philadelphia.

1804 Meriwether Lewis and William Clark explore the American West (to 1806).

1813 The Australian Blue Mountains crossed for the first time.

BOOKS
Captain Cook's *A Voyage Towards the South Pole and Round the World* (1777); David Collins' *An Account of the English Colony in New South Wales* (1798); *Rip van Winkle* by Washington Irving (1809).

THEATRE AND MUSIC
1791 *The Death Song of an Indian Chief* is the first orchestral score to be printed in the USA.

1815 Samuel Drake takes the first American theatrical company out west to Kansas.

WOMAN'S WAY Explorers Lewis and Clark used Sacagawea, a American Indian woman, as their expedition guide.

1777 Stars and Stripes adopted as the American national flag.

1783 Society of the Cincinnati, the first ex-servicemen's association, founded in New York.

1784 First Methodist ministers ordained.

1785 Benjamin Franklin invents bi-focal spectacles.

1789 Bourbon whiskey is first distilled.

1798 John Chapman ('Johnny Appleseed') plants his first apple-seed nursery.

ECO-WARRIOR John Chapman (left) helped to spread apple cultivation throughout the Ohio Valley.

1801 Merino sheep introduced to North America.

1804 First California orange grove planted.

1806 American-born Count Rumford invents the coffee percolator.

1807 Fruit-flavoured carbonated soft drinks first manufactured, in Philadelphia.

First fur-trading post established in Montana.

1808 Shakers establish a colony in Indiana.

1811 First steamboat travels on a western river, the Ohio, and covers 700 miles (1126 km).

1812 Last Indian fight in Indiana territory.

First cabin built in Wyoming.

1814 First British missionaries reach New Zealand.

First white woman arrives in Oregon Territory.

First muskets given to the New Zealand Maori, leading to many wars.

1815 – 1850

WORLD EVENTS

1815 Napoleon defeated at Waterloo.

1818 Shaka founds Zulu kingdom.

49th Parallel established as US-Canadian border.

1819 USA purchases Florida.

1820 Death of George III. Prince Regent succeeds as George IV (to 1830).

TREATY Despite the Treaty of Waitangi (1840), peace between Maori and white was unsettled.

1822 Brazil declares independence from Portuguese rule.

1830 William IV becomes King of Britain.

1832 First major reform of British Parliament.

EMPEROR Pedro II, Brazil's second emperor, succeeded to the throne on the abdication of his father, Pedro I.

1833 Slavery abolished in the British Empire.

1835 Boers begin Great Trek to escape British rule (to 1839).

1837 Victoria succeeds to the British throne.

LEISURE AND LEARNING

1818 First school established in North Dakota.

1819 *The Missouri Intelligencer*, first newspaper west of St Louis, established at Franklin, Missouri.

1821 Alphabet invented for Cherokee language.

William Becknell opens Santa Fe Trail.

1828 *American Dictionary of the English Language* published by Noah Webster.

Cherokee Phoenix of Oklahoma is first Indian-language newspaper.

1829 First Sunday School established in Texas.

PORTRAIT OF POWER A painting of an American Indian.

1830 First school opened in Iowa.

1831-6 Voyage of the *Beagle* accompanied by Charles Darwin.

1832 Mississippi source discovered.

1837 Morse code invented in USA.

1840 Budgerigars introduced from Australia to UK.

1841 University degrees granted to women in the USA.

BOOKS
The Last of the Mohicans by James Fenimore Cooper (1826); *Domestic Manners of the Americans* by Mrs Frances Trollope (1832); *The Backwoods of Canada* by Catherine Traill (1836).

LIFESTYLE CHANGES

1822 Honey bees introduced into Australia.

1823 Sour mash whiskey developed in Kentucky.

1824 Bureau of Indian Affairs set up under US War Department.

First whites executed for killing American Indians.

1827 First sawmill in the north-west

**AMERICAN ICONS
A Colt revolver dating from 1836. Right: An 1845 George Washington 10¢ stamp.**

EASY SAILING Steam-powered vessels like the *Sirius* could offer services tied to regular timetables.

established at Fort Vancouver.

1828 First settlers to journey overland from California to Oregon slaughtered by Indians.

1830 First covered wagons cross the Rockies.

1833 Potato introduced to Idaho.

1835 Samuel Colt patents a pistol with a revolving chamber.

1847 Mormons found Salt Lake City.

1849 Safety pin patented in New York.

1850 First Wellington-Auckland overland link established in New Zealand.

1851 Gold rush in Victoria, Australia.

1854 Gold miners' rebellion at Eureka Stockade, Australia.

1857 Gold discovered at Fraser River, British Columbia.

1857-65 US and UK linked by Atlantic cable.

1858 Ottawa becomes capital of Canada.

1859 Gold discovered

SUPREME SACRIFICE America's Civil War cost more lives than any of her conflicts overseas – before or since.

at Denver, Colorado.

First oil well discovered in USA.

1860 Maori revolt in New Zealand (to 1870).

1861-5 Civil war in United States.

1863 Abraham Lincoln proclaims the end of slavery in USA.

1864 Red Cross founded.

1865 Assassination of Abraham Lincoln.

Ku Klux Klan founded in Tennessee.

1867 USA buys Alaska from Russia for $7 200 000.

AFTERMATH **The gunfight at the Eureka Stockade confirmed Australian dislike of British rule.**

British North American colonies confederate as Canada and achieve self-government.

1868 Transportation of convicts to Australia ends.

1869 First coast-to-coast railway link completed in USA.

1870 First métis rising in western Canada.

1851 First recorded use of the phrase 'Go West, Young Man'.

1853 Willamette University, Oregon, becomes the first university to be established west of the Rockies.

Adelaide University founded.

First American kindergarten established at Watertown, Wisconsin.

1856 Playwright and actor Dion Boucicault, with a group of other writers, is responsible for the first copyright law for drama being introduced in the USA.

1858 Artist Thomas Baines accompanies Dr Livingstone's expedition to explore the Zambezi River.

1861 The Melbourne Cup horse race is run for the first time.

BOOKS
Moby Dick by Herman Melville (1851); *Uncle Tom's Cabin* by Harriet Beecher Stowe (1851-2); *The Female Emigrants' Guide* by Catherine Traill (1854); *The Song of Hiawatha* by H.W. Longfellow (1855); *Leaves of*

Grass by Walt Whitman; David Livingstone's *Missionary Travels in South Africa* (1857); Charles Darwin's *The Origin of Species* (1859); *A First Year in Canterbury Settlement* by Samuel Butler (1863); *The Luck of Roaring Camp* by Bret Harte; *Bush Ballads and Galloping Rhymes* by Adam Lindsay Gordon (1870).

WALT WHITMAN **The American poet, famous for his collected works** *Leaves of Grass.*

1851 Singer sewing machine introduced.

1853 Levi Strauss popularises jeans among California goldminers.

Yellow fever kills 11 000 at New Orleans.

1854 Paraffin lamp invented.

First railway opened in Argentina.

1855 Anti-Chinese riots in Tacoma, Washington.

1856 Esperanza, first Argentine agricultural colony established.

1857 Italian honeybees imported to establish honey industry in California.

1858 Invention of Mason jar

POSTHASTE **A Pony Express rider.**

revolutionises home preserving.

1859 Rabbits imported into Australia.

1860 First Dry Martini concocted in San Francisco.

Pony Express mail service starts.

1865 Welsh begin settlement of Chubut valley, Argentina.

1866 Texas closes bars and saloons on Sundays.

1867 First barbed wire patented in Ohio.

First shipment of Texas longhorns reaches Abilene.

1868 Tabasco sauce first sold in New Orleans.

Ice-cream soda invented in San Antonio.

1869 First railway bridge constructed over the Missouri river.

BARBED WIRE **Gidden's barbed wire. The manufacturer sold five times more wire than competitors.**

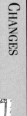

1871 – 1890

WORLD EVENTS

1871 Unification of Germany.

Siege of Paris and suppression of Paris Commune.

1872 Britain introduces voting by secret ballot.

MINES Cecil Rhodes bought the Kimberley and De Beers mines with the world's biggest cheque.

Brooklyn Bridge opened.

1875 Captain Matthew Webb first to swim the English Channel.

1876 General Custer loses the Battle of the Little Big Horn.

1877 Queen Victoria is made Empress of India.

1880 Australian bushranger Ned Kelly captured and hanged.

1881 Tsar Alexander II of Russia assassinated.

1883 Mount Krakatoa in Java erupts.

1884 Berlin Conference defines colonial frontiers in Africa.

1886 Gold discovered in South Africa.

BROKEN MAN As the buffalo disappeared, Cree chief Big Bear (centre) tried to negotiate better terms for his people.

Statue of Liberty erected in New York.

Canadian Pacific Railway completed.

1887 Queen Victoria celebrates her Golden Jubilee.

LEISURE AND LEARNING

1874 Adelaide University founded.
1876 Alexander Graham Bell invents the telephone.
1880 National Gallery of Canada established in Ottawa.

The tango emerges in the dance-halls of Buenos Aires; within a few years it becomes fashionable in North America and Europe.

1881 First tobogganing club established, in Montreal.

First major geological survey of the Grand Canyon made.

1882 Oscar Wilde tours the USA and Canada.

Australia beats England at cricket.

1883 William Cody (Buffalo Bill) organises his Wild West show.

First baseball game played under electric lights at Fort Wayne, Indiana.

Australian soprano, Nellie Melba (Helen Porter Mitchell) appears in Sydney to international acclaim.

1890 Tasmania University founded.

BOOKS
Mark Twain's *Roughing It* (1872); Jose Fernandez's *Home on the Range* (1873); Mark Twain's *Adventures of Tom Sawyer* (1875); John Nobles'

A Descriptive Handbook of the Cape Colony (1875); Olive Schreiner's *Life on an African Farm* (1883); Rolf Boldrewood's *Old Melbourne Memories* (1884); Rider Haggard's *King Solomon's Mines* (1885).

THEATRE AND MUSIC David Belasco's *The Passion Play*; Augustus Thomas's *The Burglar* (1889); Bronson Howard's *Shenandoah* (1889).

MISSISSIPPI BOY Novelist and travel writer Mark Twain as a 24-year-old river pilot.

LIFESTYLE CHANGES

THE SINGING WIRE Australian engineers laying the Overland Telegraph in 1872.

1872 Canada passes Dominions Land Act to grant free land to pioneers.

Overland telegraph line links Australia to outside world.

1873 Royal Canadian Mounted Police (Mounties) formed.

1875 Canned baked beans first produced, in Portland, Maine.

1876 Melville Bissell of Michigan perfects carpet sweeper.

Henry Heinz bottles tomato ketchup.

Sir Henry Wickham smuggles rubber-tree seeds out of Brazil.

Australia and New Zealand joined by telegraph cable.

1881 Last major cattle drive in USA.

1884 Washington conference standardises time zones based on Greenwich in England.

1886 Coca-Cola launched as 'Esteemed Brain Tonic and Intellectual Beverage'.

1871 The toilet roll is invented.

Brazil passes The Law of the Free Womb.

CANNED CATTLE Beef extract and corned beef from North and South America became popular foods.

1891 – 1914

1891-1905 Trans-Siberian Railway built.

1893 World Exhibition in Chicago.

1895 X-rays discovered.

Marconi invents radio telegraphy.

1896 First modern Olympic Games held in Athens.

1897 Queen Victoria's Diamond Jubilee.

Klondike gold rush begins.

1898 Spanish-American war. Spain cedes Cuba, Puerto Rico, Guam and the Philippines for $20 000 000.

Paris Metro opened.

CAPTURED A blindfolded Boer is made a prisoner-of-war.

1899-1902 War between Boers and British in South Africa.

1900-1 Commonwealth of Australia created.

Anti-foreign Boxer Rising in China.

1903 Wright brothers achieve powered flight.

1905 Abortive revolution in Russia.

1906 Earthquake in San Francisco kills 700.

1911 Roald Amundsen reaches South Pole.

1912 SS *Titanic* sinks on her maiden voyage, drowning 1513.

1914 Outbreak of First World War.

1891 Carnegie Music Hall opened in New York.

1892 Basketball developed at YMCA, in Springfield, Massachusetts.

1893 First Ferris Wheel erected at Chicago Exposition.

1906 The springbok used as emblem of the South African rugby team.

1911 First Hollywood film studio established.

SPRINGBOK The South African gazelle became the symbol of its rugby team.

First Indianapolis 500 motor race.

BOOKS
F.J. Turner's *The Significance of the Frontier in American History* (1893); Theodore Roosevelt's *The Winning of the West* (1896); Euclides da Cunha's *Rebellion in the Backlands (Os Sertoes)* (1902); Owen Whistler's *The Virginian* (1902); Andy Adams's *The Log of a Cowboy* (1903); Jack London's *Call of the Wild* (1903); Joseph Murphy's *Such Is Life* (1903); Robert M. Service's *Song of a Sourdough* (1907); Lucy M. Montgomery's *Anne of Green Gables* (1908); Willa Cather's *O, Pioneers!* (1913).

CHRONICLERS OF THE WILD American writers Willa Cather (left) wrote of pioneer fortitude, Jack London (right) of the savagery of the wilderness.

THEATRE AND MUSIC
James A. Herne's *Shore Acres* (1892); Augustus Thomas's *In Mizzoura* (1893); Clyde Fitch's *The Girl with the Green Eyes* (1902); *Alexander's Ragtime Band* by Irving Berlin (1911).

1891 Dial telephone invented in Kansas City.

Burroughs patents adding machine in St Louis.

First electric kettle marketed.

1892 First concrete road made for Main Street, Bellefontaine in Ohio.

1893 New Zealand women get vote.

1895 King C. Gillette invents the safety razor.

BIRTH OF A LEGEND Director Cecil B. De Mille (far left) with the cast of *The Squaw Man*, 1913.

1896 Ice-cream cone invented.

1897 First Women's Institute meets in Stoney Creek, Ontario.

1898 Corn Flakes first made by the Kellogg brothers in Michigan.

1898-9 Dhoukobors settle in Saskatchewan.

1900 8000 die in Texas hurricane.

1901 Mombasa to Lake Victoria railway completed.

1902 First window envelopes made in Springfield, Massachusetts.

1903 First coast-to-coast crossing of America made by car.

1904 Women in South Australia get the vote.

1906 Milk cartons pioneered in San Francisco.

1907 Mother's Day established in Philadelphia.

First electric washing machines manufactured in Chicago.

1908 First Model T Ford manufactured.

INDEX

ACKNOWLEDGMENTS

ABBREVIATIONS
T = Top; M = Middle; B = Bottom;
R = Right; L = Left.
ATL= Alexander Turnbull Library, Auckland.
BAL = Bridgeman Art Library, London.
BBHC = Buffalo Bill Historical Centre, Wyoming.
ETA = E T Archive, London.
MA = Museum Africa, New Town, South Africa.
MEPL = Mary Evans Picture Library, London.
NLA = National Library of Australia, Canberra.
PNP = Peter Newark's Pictures, Bath.
RB = Range/Bettmann, London.
TBA = Toucan Books Archive, London.

1 *Hand-Cart*/PNP. 2-3 *Advice on the Prairie*, William Ranney/BAL. 4 *Halt of a Boer's Family*/BAL, TL; *Rundle Street, Adelaide*, Samuel Thomas, Library of South Australia/ETA. 5 *Detail of Pigeon Egg Head*, George Catlin, Smithsonian Institute, Washington/TBA, TL; *Frontispiece of Geography Book*/TBA, TR; *Landing Passengers in Buenos Aires*/TBA, MR; *Convicts in Tasmania*/MEPL, BL; *Advert*/TBA, BR. 6 *Cartoon*, by Cruikshank, William Fehr Collection, Cape Town. 7 *The Landing of the British Settlers in Algoa Bay, in the Year 1820*, Thomas Baines, from the permanent collection of the King George VI Art Gallery, Port Elizabeth, South Africa, T; *Below Deck on a Troop Ship Bound for the Cape in 1819*, R Dingley, Cape Archives Depot, B; *John Curry Sod House, Custer Country, Nebraska, 1886*, Solomon D Butcher Collection, Nebraska State Historical Society (ref: B 983-1048), T; MEPL, B. 9 *Sophie's Whare and the Temperance Hotel after the Tarawera Eruption in 1886*, Burton Brothers, Museum of New Zealand Te Papa Tongewera, T; The Massillon Museum, Ohio, B. 10 *Natives of Port Lincoln* W Westall/ETA, L; *Indian Family, Brazil*/Popperfoto, R. 11 *Union Pacific Locomotive, Utah*, 1869/PNP. 12 *Buffalo Bill Poster*, Dr Richard Slatta, T; *Voortrekkers*, Transvaal Archives Depot, B.13 *The Promised Land: The Grayson Family*, William S Jewett, Berry-Hill Galleries, New York. 14 *Trap and Snow Shoes*, BBHC, L; *A Hudson Bay Trapper*, Olaf C Seltzer, Thomas Gilcrease Institute of American History and Art, Tulsa, Oklahoma, R. 15 *Fur Trappers Resting*/PNP, T; *Beaver Hats*/TBA, BL; *The Old Trapper*, McCord Museum of Canadian History, Notman Photographic Archives, Montreal, BR. 18 *Man fighting off a Bear*, Bancroft Library, University of California, T; *The Trappers' Return*, George Caleb Bingham, Detroit Institute of Arts Founder Society, B; *Lewis*/RB, TL; *Clark*/RB, TR; *Condor*, American Philosophical Society, Philadelphia, B. 20 *Indian Trapper Family*/TBA, T; *Trading Token*/TBA, M; *Log Cabin*/RB, B. 21 *Fiddler*, George Caleb Bingham, Nelson-Atkins Museum of Art, Kansas City, T; *Lumbering*/RB, B. 22 *New England Farmhouse*/PNP. 23 Illustration by Gill Tomblin. 24 *Starving Family*/RB. 25 *Hog Butchering*/PNP, TL; *Wild Turkey*/PNP, TR; *Maple Sugaring*, N Currier/PNP, B. 26 *The Pioneer*, from *Harpers Weekly*, 1868/PNP, T; *Making Cherry Bounce*, Lewis Miller, Historical Society of York County, PA, B. 27 *Wheelbarrow*/TBA, L; *Settlers' Home*/RB, R. 28 *A Surround of Buffalo by Indians*, Alfred Jacob Miller, BBHC. 29 *Dead Buffalo*, Montana Historical Society, Helena, MT, T; *Buffalo Skull*, BBHC, B. 30 *Mission San Gabriel* F Deppe, Santa Barbara Mission Archives Library, T; *Independence, Missouri: Courthouse*, US Library of Congress, B. 31 *Advert*, US Library of Congress, TL; *Pioneer Wagon*/RB, B. 32/33 Illustration by Gill Tomblin. 34 *Quinine Bottle*/TBA, TL; *Cholera Poster*/TBA, TR; *An Attack on an Emigrant Train*, Charles Wimar, University of Michigan, Museum of Art, B. 35 *George Catlin*, William Frisk, 1849/RB, T; *Comanche Feats of Horsemanship*, George Catlin/PNP, B. 36 *Interior of Fort Laramie*, Alfred Jacob Miller, Walters Art Gallery, Baltimore. 36-37 *Geronimo and his Band of Apache Renegades*, 1886, US Library of Congress, B. 37 *General Custer*/PNP, T. 38 *A Cavalryman's Breakfast on the Plains*, Frederick Remington/PNP. 39 *10th Cavalry Escort to General Merrit, St Mary's, Montana*, 1894, Montana Historical Society, Helena, MT, T; *Mule*/TBA, B. 40-41 *Storm in the Rocky Mountains*, Albert Bierstadt, Brooklyn Museum, New York. 42 *Union Pacific Poster*/PNP, TL; *Railroad Building, Burlington Northern Railroad*, TR. 42-43 *Sod-House*, Solomon D Butcher Collection, Nebraska State Historical Society (ref: B 983-1653). 44 *Kitchen Implements*, BBHC, T; *Pioneer Woman*/PNP, B. 45 Nebraska State Historical Society, L; RB, R. 46 *Cartoon*, US Library of Congress, T; *Chinese Laundry*, Idaho State Historical Society (ref: 83-37.22), B. 47 *Placer Mining*, Haynes Foundation Collection, Montana Historical Society, Helena, MT, L; *Panning for Gold*/PNP, R. 48 *A Goldminers' Ball*/PNP, T; *Oscar Wilde*/RB, B; *Cowboy*/ PNP, T; *Cowboy Hat and Spurs*, BBHC, BL; *Saddle*, Colorado Historical Society, Denver, BR. 50 *Early Cattle Ranch*, Brown Brothers, T; *Trailing Cattle to Abeline*, Frederick Remington/PNP, B. 51 *Women Branding Cattle*, Colorado Historical Society, Denver, T; *The Rabbit Hole Springs*, from a sketch by J G Bruff/TBA, B. 52 *Barkerville*, Provincial Archives of British Columbia, Victoria. 53 *Methodist Camp Meeting*/RB, T; *Methodist Circuit Rider*/PNP, B. 54 *Woman's Holy War*/BAL, T; *Shakers Dancing*/PNP, BL; *Shaker Chair*, 1810-20/BAL, BR. 55 *Brigham Young*, c1851/PNP, T; *Great Salt Lake City*, I N Phelps Stokes Collection, Miriam and Ira D Wallach Division of Art, Prints and Photographs, New York Public Library, Astor, Lenox and Tilden Foundations, B. 56 *Mormon Family*/RB. 57 *Sunday Morning in the Mines*, Karl Nahl, E B Crocker Art Gallery, Sacramento, California/BAL, T; *Anti-Chinese Riot*, Denver/PNP, B. 58 *Man Hanging from Tree*, BBHC (ref: B. 71. 717.1), T; *Highway Robber*, 1879, Wells Fargo Bank, B. 59 *Handcuffs and Gun*, BBHC, TL; Wells Fargo Bank, TR; *Vigilante Certificate*, Bancroft Library, University of California, B. 60 *Mullinville*, Kansas, 1885, Kansas State Historical Society, Topeka, Kansas, T; *View of St Louis, Missouri, from Lucas Place*, Edward Sachse and Co, Chicago Historical Society, B. 61 *Advert Cartoon for Railway Depot Lunchroom*, US Library of Congress. 62 *'Herald' Office*, Colin Taylor, Hastings, T; *Advert from a Sears Roebuck Catalogue*, 1902/ PNP, BL; *Stove*/TBA, BR. 63 *Advert for South Dakota*/TBA. 64 *Market Scene, Sansome Street, San Francisco*, William Hahn, Crocker Art Museum, Sacramento, T; *Prostitute*, Providence Public Library, Rhode Island, B. 65 *The Crow Family in Montana*, Smithsonian Institute, Washington. 66 *Reverend Duncan*, Provincial Archives of British Columbia, Victoria, BL; *Women Spinning*, Provincial Archives of British Columbia, Victoria, BR. 66-67 *New Westminster*, Provincial Archives of British Columbia, Victoria. 67 *Gabriel Dumont*, Glenbow Archives, Calgary, Alberta. 68 *North-West Mounted Police*, Royal Canadian Mounted Police, Regina, Saskatchewan. 69 *Immigrants*, Ernest Brown Photographic Collection, Provincial Archives of Alberta (ref: B 5628), T; *Poster*/PNP, B. 70 *Gauchos from Vidal's Views in Buenos Aries and Monte Video*, Dr Richard Slatta, North Carolina State University. 71 Map. 72 Dr Richard Slatta, North Carolina State University, B. 73 *Pampas Indians*/TBA, T; *Saladero*/TBA, B. 74 *Tavern Scene*, Dr Richard Slatta, North Carolina State University, T; *Horse Race*, Newberry Library/Dr Richard Slatta, North Carolina State University, B. 75 *Welsh Farm in Patagonia*, Glyn Williams, Anglesey, T; *Train*/Hulton Deutsch, B. 76 *Estancia Owner*/TBA, T; *Estancia*/Popperfoto, B. 77 *Wealthy Women*/TBA. 78 *Buenos Aires*/Roger-Viollet, Paris, T; *Street Vendor*/TBA, B. 79 *Prinz Maximillian zu Wied-Neuwied in Brazilian Costume*, Johann Heinrich Richter/AKG; *Indians from Viagem Filosofica*, Alexandre Rodrigues Ferreira, University of London Library, B. 80 *Rain Forest Scene*/AKG. 81 *Bird from Viagem Filosofica*, University of London Library, T; *Lady in Sedan*/BAL, B. 82 *Indian with Rubber Tube*/TBA, T; *Photographs of Rubber Production*, Icongraphia, Brazil. 83 *Manaus Opera House*, Icongraphia, Brazil, T; *Coffee Workers*, H Hoffenburg, New York, B. 84 *Hatmaker*, H Hoffenburg, New York, T; *Rio de Janeiro*/Hulton Deutsch, B. 85 *First Night in the Colony*, artist unknown, Ballarat Art Gallery, Victoria. 86 *Party of Soldiers Visiting Botany Bay*, British Museum/ETA. 87 *Warriors of New South Wales*, J H Clark/ETA, T; *Map of Australia*, B. 88 *Convict Notice*/TBA, TL; *Convict Ship*/Hulton Deutsch, TM; *Convict Leg Irons*/Hulton Deutsch, TR. 89 *View from the Summit of Mount York: Convicts Stone-Breaking*, Augustus Earle, The Rex Nan Kivell Collection, NLA (ref: NK12/23). 90 *The Flogging of Greenwood*, Image Library, State Library of New South Wales, T; *A Government Jail Gang*, Augustus Earle, NLA, B. 91 *Cartoon, Emigration in Search of a Husband*, The Rex Nan Kivell Collection, NLA (ref: NK 1616), T; *Mary Haydock*, Image Library, State Library of New South Wales, B. 92 *Sydney from St Leonard's Road, North Shore*, Thomas Baines, Royal Geographical Society/BAL. 93 *Natives of New South Wales on the Streets of Sydney*, Augustus Earle/ETA, T; *Topsy Turvey*, John Leech, Rex Nan Kivell Collection, NLA (ref: NK 5618/11), B. 94 *Poster*/TBA, L; *Land Sales from Urana, New South Wales*, *Illustrated Sydney News*, 1876, NLA, R. 95 *Kangaroo*/MEPL, T; *Platypuses*, Natural History Museum Photo Library, B. 96 *Bringing Down the Wool from a Murray Station*, Edward Roper/ETA, T; *Sheep Dipping*, Image Library, State Library of New South Wales, B. 97 *Shearing the Rams*, Tom Roberts, Felton Bequest, 1932, National Gallery of Victoria, Melbourne. 98 *Farmer*, State Library of Victoria, T; *Bushmen Watering Horses in the Desert*, detail, George Hamilton/ETA, B. 99 *Pioneer Family*, Image Library, State Library of New South Wales, L; *Australia: News from Home*, George Baxter, Maidstone Museum and Art Gallery, Kent/BAL, R. 100 *Ned Kelly*/ETA, L; *Ned Kelly*/MEPL, R. 101 *Police and Aboriginals Clash*, G C Mundy, Royal Commonwealth Society Collection, Cambridge University Library, T; *Jenny*, Image Library, State Library of New South Wales, B. 102 *Goldmining*/ETA, T; *Panning for Gold*/Popperfoto, B. 103 *View of Melbourne Across The Yarra*, Henry Gritten, Christie's/BAL. 104 *Demonstration from Illustrated Sydney News*, National Library of Australia, L; *Philip Street*, Sydney, Image Library, State Library of New South Wales, R. 105 *Reading Room*, Melbourne Public Library, La Trobe Collection, State Library of Victoria, T; *A Homestead, Mitcham*, James Shaw/BAL, BL; *Anthony Trollope*, S Laurence, National Portrait Gallery, London, BR. 106 *Picnic Party at Hanging Rock near Mount Macedon*, William Ford, National Gallery of Victoria, Melbourne. 107 *Sunday at the Diggings*/MEPL, T; *Father O'Donovan Visits the New Catholic Church at Gulgong, 1872*, Image Library, State Library of New South Wales, B. 108 *Melbourne Cup Ticket*, 1899/TBA, TL; *McClaren's Boxing Saloon, Main Road, Ballarat*, S T Gill, 1854, Rex Nan Kivell Collection, NLA (ref: NK 1409), TR; *Hyde Park, Sydney*, Image Library, State Library of New South Wales, BR; *Portrait of Nannultera*, J M Crossland, NLA (ref: NK 6295), BR. 109 *Aboriginals,Coolgardie*, Battye Library Pictorial Collection, Perth (ref: 20 147 P). 110 *Lake Wakatipu with Mount Earnslaw, Middle Island, New Zealand*, Eugene Von Guerard, Auckland City Art Gallery. 111 *Whaling*/TBA, T. 112 *View of Taupiri Village and Plain from the Top of Little Taupiri Hill*, Alfred Sharpe, Auckland City Art Gallery. 113 *The Descent of the Miko Cliff, 106 feet, Middle Island*, Charles Heaphy, British Library. 114 *Advert*, TBA, T; *SS Grafton at Jackson's Bay*, West Coast Historical Museum, Hotitika, New Zealand (ref: 2147), B. 115 *A Digger on the Tramp*, R C Reid, Making New Zealand Collection/ATL (ref: F 615916 1/2), T; Pioneer Library Archives, Greymouth, South Island, B. 116 *A Family and Their House*, ATL (ref: G 65619 1/2), T; Collection of Hawkes Bay Cultural Trust, Hawkes Bay Museum, Napier, New Zealand (ref: 7453), B. 117 *Opawa Station, Albury*, James Preston, Canterbury Museum, Christchurch, T; *The Camp, the Cook and the Cabbage*, ATL (ref: F22483 1/2), B. 118 *Cooker*/TBA, T; *The Bronden House near Wanganui*, 1907, F J Denton Collection/ATL (ref: 16786 1/1), B. 119 *Picnic*, ATL (ref: G16265 1/1). 120 *Interior of a Maori Pa in the Olden Time*, Sam Stuart, Auckland City Art Gallery, T; *Te Kuha*, Horatio Robley, Museum of New Zealand Te Papa Tongarewa, Wellington (ref: B 15661 (CT), B. 121 *A Settler Bartering Tobacco for Potatoes and Pumpkin*, J A Gilfillan, Hocken Library, University of Otago, Dunedin, T; *La Venus au Mouillage de Otaiti*, Louis Le Breton, ATL, B. 122 *Kauri Forest, Wairoa River, Kaipara*, Charles Heaphy, ATL, T; *Kiwi and Moa*/TBA, B. 123 *An Incident During a Hau-Hau Raid on a Settler's Farm*, Gustavus Ferdinand von Tempsky, Hocken Library, University of Otago, Dunedin, L; *Notice*/TBA, R. 124 *Wesleyn Mission Station at Waingaroa: Natives Assembling to Worship*, George Baxter, London Wesleyn Missionary Society, ATL, T; *Hami Hone Ropiha (John Hobbs)*, William Ewart, Ngati Kahunguru, oil on canvas, Auckland City Art Gallery Collection, presented Sir George Grey, 1887, B. 125 *Baptism of the Maori Chief, Te Puni, Otaki Church*, Rex Nan Kivell Collection, NLA (ref: NK1103), L; *Maori New Testament*, 1837, ATL, R. 126 *Maori Family by a Pataka*, Burton Brothers, Museum of New Zealand Te Papa Tongarewa, Wellington. 127 *Cradock's Pass between George and Longkloof in the 1840s*, Cape Archives Depot (ref: M429). 128 *Inanda Kreal, Natal*, G F Angus, MA (ref: 5099). 129 *Nazea, a Malay Woman in her Walking Costume*, MA, L; *A Baker Assisted by his Dog*, Sir Charles D'Oyly, MA (ref: 74/2539), R; 130 *Interior of a Trekboer Tent in Griqueland*, Charles Bell, MA (ref: 244), T. 130 The National Cultural History Museum, Pretoria, BR. 131 *Boer Huntsman*, Samuel Deniell, MA (ref: 65/4005), T; *Boers Returning from a Hunt*, Samuel Daniell, MA (ref: 2313), B. 134 *Interior of the Farm of Louis Pretorius*, T. Baines, MA (ref: 596), T; *Burghers Encamped Outside the Dutch Reformed Church, Pretoria*, National Cultural History Museum, Pretoria, B. 135 *A Hottentot Herdsman*, G F Angus, MA (ref: 50865). 136 *After the Hunt - a Bushman Cave Painting*, Thomas Baines, MA (ref: 564), T; *Bushmen Driving Cattle up a Kloof, Boers in Pursuit*, C P Bell, MA (ref: 564), B. 137 *Old Danster, a Grique or Coranna Chief near Koesberg*, Charles Bell, MA (ref: 2465). 138 *Landing of the British Settlers in Algoa Bay*, Thomas Baines, from Jane Carruther's *Thomas Baines: Eastern Cape Sketches, 1848 to 1852*, © The Brenthurst Press, 1990, Plate 9. 139 *Interior of a Wealthy Settler's Home (Probably Pigot Park) in the 1820s*, Cape Archives Depot, T; *Grahamstown in 1823*, unknown artist, The Albany Museum, Grahamstown, B; 140 *Procession on the Anniversary of the Slaves' Liberation, Cape Town*, George Duft, MA (ref: 71/534). 141 *A Canteen Scene During the Frontier Wars*, W H F L Langschmidt, William Fehr Collection. 142 *Battle of Blauwkrantz*, Thomas Baines, MA. 142-143 *Battle of Blood River*, W H Coetzer, Voortrekker Museum, Pietermaritzburg. 143 *Mimuni, Nephew of Shaka*, G F Angus, MA, T. 144 *Rhinoceros Hunt*, Yves, MA (ref: 71/2160), T; MEPL, B. 145 *Ivory and Curios in the Grahamstown Market Place*, Thomas Baines, The Albany Museum, Grahamstown, T; Hulton Deutsch, B. 146 *Bound for the Goldfields*, 1894, MA, T; *A Group Returning Home*, Thomas Baines, MA (ref: 6332), B. 147 McGregor Museum, Kimberley. 148 Popperfoto, T; Transvaal Archives, Pretoria (ref: 22495), B. 149 Hulton Deutsch. 150 Hulton Deutsch, T; PNP, MR; TBA, ML, B. 151 British Library, TL; William Fehr Collection, Cape Town, TR; PNP, M, B. 152 New Zealand High Commission/BAL, T; MEPL, ML; Smithsonian Institute, MR; TBA, BL; Hulton Deutsch, BR. 153 MEPL, TR; Chicago Historical Society (ref: AHD 243x), TL; PNP, BR. 154 TBA, TR; De Beers Consolidated Mines, TL; RB, M; *Overland Telegraph Party*, Image Library, State Library of New South Wales, BL; Robert Opie Collection, BR. 155 Hulton Deutsch, T; RB, ML, MR; Springbok, TBA, BL; The Kobal Collection, B.

Front cover: PNP, TL, BL; Berry-Hill Galleries, New York, MM; Nelson-Atkins Museum of Art, Kansas City, BR; TBA, BM; RB, ML.

Back cover: TBA, TL, TR; Santa Barbara Mission Archives Library, M; BBHC, BR; PNP, BL.